THE **BIBLE** IN 90 DAYS™

90

PARTICIPANT'S GUIDE

TED COOPER JR. WITH STEPHEN AND AMANDA SORENSON

AN EXTRAORDINARY EXPERIENCE WITH THE WORD OF GOD

THE **BIBLE** IN 90 DAYS™

PARTICIPANT'S GUIDE

TED COOPER JR. WITH **STEPHEN** AND **AMANDA SORENSON**

ZONDERVAN™

GRAND RAPIDS, MICHIGAN 49530 USA

We want to hear from you. Please send your comments about this book to us in care of zreview@zondervan.com. Thank you.

ZONDERVAN™

The Bible in 90 Days™ Participant's Guide
Copyright © 2005 by Theodore W. Cooper Jr.
"The Bible in 90 Days" is a trademark of Bible in 90 Days.

Requests for information should be addressed to:

Zondervan, *Grand Rapids, Michigan 49530*

ISBN-10: 0-310-26684-X
ISBN-13: 978-0-310-26684-6

Bible Background Sources:

Zondervan Handbook to the Bible, © 1999 Pat and David Alexander.

Zondervan NIV Study Bible, Copyright © 1985, 1995, 2002 by The Zondervan Corporation.

You Are Here in the Bible, Copyright © 2001, 2002, 2003 by Ted Cooper Jr.

Interior design by Beth Shagene

Printed in the United States of America

06 07 08 09 10 11 • 17 16 15 14 13 12 11 10 9 8 7 6 5 4 3 2

CONTENTS

WELCOME TO THE BIBLE IN 90 DAYS™

You are about to embark on a special journey.

The journey will start on the first page of the Bible and end on the last. You'll read 12 pages a day and finish in 90 days.

Others will be on this journey with you. You'll gather with them once a week to ask questions, share insights, and hear a lesson drawn from your reading. You'll encourage them and they'll encourage you.

I took this journey for the first time six years ago. In the beginning, I was agnostic. Halfway through, I became a believer. Your experience will differ from mine, because you won't start this journey with the same background or needs. But whatever your background, be prepared for an extraordinary experience.

Reading every word of the Bible is not the norm, nor is doing so in such a brief period of time. Something just happens when you do this. In your case, this "something" might be obvious, or maybe it won't become apparent for a while.

This curriculum and its accompanying resources will continue to evolve, so we invite your suggestions and comments. We've always believed that a critical ingredient in this curriculum's effectiveness is the godly guidance we receive from its participants and leaders … people like you.

Please let us hear from you, either during or after your journey. We'll be praying for you.

Blessings,

Ted

Ted Cooper Jr.
Creator, *The Bible in 90 Days*™
(713)526-6800
www.biblein90days.org/support/

FREQUENTLY ASKED QUESTIONS

Over time, a number of frequently asked questions have surfaced regarding this Bible reading program. Here are some of the more common queries and answers:

Q:Should I do anything before I start reading each day?
A: We recommend that you say a brief, silent prayer such as this: "Gracious Father, thank you for the gift I hold in my hands. May your Spirit fill me and interpret your precious words for me as I read. In your Son's name I pray, Amen."

Q:How much will I read each day?
A: Each day you'll read twelve pages in the *NIV Bible in 90 Days*. On day one you start with page 1, on day two you pick up where you left off. At the end of 90 days, you'll have read the Bible from cover to cover.

Q:When should I read?
A: That's completely up to you. Some will read first thing in the morning, before getting out of bed. Others will make it the last thing they do each night. Still others will read at various points in between. Some will read their daily quota all in one sitting. Others will space their reading throughout the day, reading a page or two in several sittings. Try more than one approach ... one of the benefits of doing this reading is becoming comfortable with reading your Bible at any time.

Q:What if I get behind?
A: Try your best not to. But, if you do, there is one VERY IMPORTANT RULE about catching up: DO *NOT* SKIP ANY PAGES. There are two reasons for this rule: (1) if you skip anything, by definition you will not have read from *cover to cover*, which is an important part of

this process; (2) if you skip anything, you are *unlikely* to go back and read what you skipped, so you won't end up reading the entire Bible, either.

If you get behind, just read some extra pages each day until you've caught back up to the group.

Q:What if I get WAY behind?

A:Set aside a large block of time during one day—Sundays are particularly good for this—and just "plow through" the reading. This may seem more like a chore than a spiritual experience, but you will probably be surprised by the insights you glean from this. As importantly, after a day (or so) of reading this way, you'll be caught up! Remember, too, that God's work sometimes seems like, well, *work*. Reading the Bible from cover to cover *is* a challenge; however, when this challenge is met, you'll be glad that you persevered.

DISCUSSION GROUP RULES OF ENGAGEMENT

1. **In each group, we've asked one or two people to serve as facilitators.** These individuals will lead or guide the discussion, but will NOT teach.

2. **Each small group member is INVITED to join in the discussion, but is NOT REQUIRED to do so.** Even if a question is posed for everyone in the group to answer (for example, "Let's go around the table and find out what everyone thinks about…"), each participant should feel free to remain silent on the subject. In such a case, someone abstaining might simply say, "Thank you, but I'd like to pass on answering that."

3. **Alternatively, please do NOT dominate the discussion.** Discussion time is limited, so please be sure that everyone who wants to speak has the opportunity to do so.

4. **Be sure to respect one another's beliefs, whether new to the Bible or a lifetime student.** We are not here to CORRECT or even GUIDE anyone's interpretation of what is being read. Rather, we are here to encourage each person as he/she struggles with its meaning.

5. **Begin and end your small group sessions—and return to the large group—promptly.**

WHOLE GROUP DISCUSSION

1. Have you ever tried to read the entire Bible before? Why or why not?

2. If you have tried to read the Bible in its entirety, what challenges did you face in fulfilling your desire? Where did you start? How far did you get?

3. What have you found to be difficult and rewarding in your attempts to read the Bible regularly?

4. If you have successfully read the entire Bible before, what were the circumstances? What motivated you to keep at it? How satisfied were you with your accomplishment?

5. If you have started to read the Bible but have never completed your reading goal, what really kept you from finishing what you started?

6. Why do you believe it is important to read the entire Bible? What do you expect to discover in terms of practical living, spiritual growth, or knowledge of history, or other areas?

7. What is most intimidating about the prospect of reading the entire Bible in 90 days?

8. What most excites you about the prospect of reading the entire Bible in 90 days?

ON YOUR OWN BETWEEN SESSIONS

This Week's Reading Tips

- Memorize your mission, which is: *to read, attentively, every word of the Bible in 90 days.*

- Don't expect to be able to consciously recall everything you read. At this point, focus on what you *can* recall and *don't worry about the rest.*

- Don't expect to understand everything you read. Pay attention to what you *do* understand and *don't worry about the rest.*

- At least once during this week, try breaking up your daily reading into two or more sessions.

Genesis Overview

Genesis is the book of beginnings and sets the stage for everything that follows in the Bible. It establishes God as the creator of all that is—in heaven, on earth, and beyond. It focuses on the essential relationship of humanity, the relationship between God and the people he created. In Genesis we see Satan entice Adam and Eve to disobey God, which establishes the central conflict of human history. The remainder of the Bible is the story of how God resolves that loss of relationship throughout human history.

Exodus Overview

Exodus is not only the story of Israel's departure from the land of Egypt, it is the story of Israel's departure from the lifestyle of Egypt. It is not merely a journey of time and distance, it is a journey of the heart as a holy God prepares his chosen people to live the life he offers in the land he has provided. What a journey it is as God reveals himself and invites his people into relationship with him!

Read This Week

Pages 1−84 of the *NIV Bible in 90 Days* (Gen. 1:1−Ex. 40:38)

Personal Progress

If it is helpful to do so, use the following chart to record your reading progress this week. Establish a reading schedule that works well for you — then stick with it. Try to make it a habit to pray before you begin reading each day, asking God to use his Word to instruct and guide you.

✓	Day	Pages from the *NIV Bible in 90 Days*	Passage begins:
	1 (Today)	1–12	Genesis 1:1
	2	12–24	Genesis 17:1
	3	24–36	Genesis 28:20
	4	36–48	Genesis 40:12
	5	48–60	Exodus 1:1
	6	60–72	Exodus 15:19
	7	72–84	Exodus 29:1

Personal Reading Notes

Take a moment to record the highlights — knowledge gained, puzzling questions, "aha! moments" — you experience during your reading this week:

Try It!

Memorize the names of the first five books of the Bible before the next session:

G_____   E_____

L_____   N_____

D_____

READING OUTLINE

Discuss Today: pages 1 – 84 of *NIV Bible in 90 Days* (Gen. 1:1 – Ex. 40:38)

Reading for the Coming Week: pages 84 – 168 of *NIV Bible in 90 Days* (Lev. 1:1 – Deut. 23:11)

SMALL GROUP DISCUSSION

Reading Follow-up

1. How was your reading this week? What challenges did you face in getting your reading done? What was the most effective thing you did to meet those challenges?

2. What kind of reading routine seems to work best for you, given your activities and schedule?

3. As you read the Bible this week, which particular thought(s) and/ or event(s) stood out to you or surprised you? Why?

4. Which question(s) came up during your reading for which you'd like to find answers?

Reading Discovery

Note: The following questions are intended to stimulate discussion. There is no need to answer them prior to your class or small group meeting.

1. In what ways did Adam and Eve's sin affect their offspring and the world in which they lived?

2. What kind of a man was Abraham? What plans did God want to accomplish through him? What did God commit himself to do? (See Gen. 12:2–3; 17:7–8.)

3. As you read about what happened to Joseph and how situations in his life worked out, what surprised you? If you were writing a novel about his life, what would you title it? Why?

4. In what ways do you think Moses changed between his time in the Egyptian court and when God spoke to him from the burning bush forty years later? What do Moses' objections to God's call to deliver Israel from bondage reveal about his insecurities and view of God? (See Ex. 3:11, 13; 4:1, 10, 13.)

5. What kind of a picture of God are you developing through your reading so far? What are some of God's characteristics and attributes, and how did he demonstrate them to his chosen people?

6. What do you think was God's purpose in providing the Israelites with so many specific instructions regarding daily life and worship? What did God demonstrate, through the tabernacle, about his commitment to be with his people?

Did You Know?

- The book of Genesis establishes four great principles that are crucial to our understanding of God's Word:

  1. God brings order out of chaos by making distinctions and setting limits.

  2. Man was created in the image and likeness of God. After the fall, he retained the image but not the likeness.

  3. Life involves choices, and choices have consequences, so choose wisely.

  4. Satan's strategy is to humanize God (doubt the Word); minimize sin (deny the Word); and deify man (replace the Word).

- The ancient Egyptians revered and worshiped many gods, including snakes. When Moses' staff miraculously became a snake that swallowed up the Egyptian magicians' snakes (Ex. 7:8–13), God demonstrated his power over the pharaoh and Egypt's gods. Furthermore, the plagues God sent to the Egyptians directly confronted and rebuked their worship of other gods. The Nile River, which turned to blood, was linked to the god Hapi. Frogs were linked to the goddess Heqt. The cows that died during the livestock plague were linked to Hathor, the cow-god; Khnum, the ram-god; and the Egyptian bull-gods Apis and Mnevis (*NIV Study Bible*, notes for Ex. 8:2, 9:3). God wanted the ancient Egyptians to realize that he alone was God Almighty, *Yahweh*, the *I AM WHO I AM* (Ex. 3:14).

- God instructed Moses to have the people build a tabernacle so that God could have a visible place to live among his people. The building and furnishing of the tabernacle utilized the people's skills in spinning, weaving, and dying fibers; embroidery; rounding, polishing, and engraving precious and semi-precious stones; gold and silver work (*Zondervan Handbook to the Bible*, 169, 174). They gladly committed their work and wealth to "God's tent," and when it was completed, the visible symbols of God's presence—his cloud by day and the fire by night—rested on the tabernacle and filled it with the light of his glory. For the next 300 years, until Solomon built the temple in Jerusalem, the tabernacle was the focus of the nation's worship (*Handbook*, 179).

Order out of chaos
  — making distinctions
  — setting limits
Man created in image + likeness
          potential,   ability to
          approximation   do something

<u>Choices have consequences</u>

<u>Exodus</u>   God's Provision

Passover

Crossover

Law

Tabernacle

VIDEO DISCUSSION (OPTIONAL)

1. As you watched the video, which particular point(s) stood out to you? Why?

2. Which aspect of the video particularly enhanced your understanding of what you read this past week?

3. What would you identify as the key themes of this portion of Scripture?

4. What impact can what you've just seen make on your life today?

This Week's Reading Tip

At least once during this week, try breaking your daily
reading routine into two or more sessions.

Leviticus Overview

Leviticus is essentially the rule book for Israel's priests. All of the
laws spring from God's covenant with his chosen people. The Hebrews
had grown up in slavery, so these laws are part of the process God used
to mold them into the people they needed to be before they entered the
Promised Land. These laws are about relationships: the relationships
they were to have with one another and the relationship they were to
have with their God. As you read, notice the unchanging character of
God and our human need for forgiveness and a restored relationship
with God. Leviticus helps us understand why we need to be holy and
why it was necessary for Jesus to stand in our place and die for our sins
(*Handbook*, 181).

Numbers Overview

The Hebrew name of the book of Numbers means "in the desert."
And that's what Numbers is all about. As the Israelites approach the
Promised Land of Canaan, they must choose whether or not to trust
their God. Notice what happens when they focus on circumstances and
feelings rather than on what God promises to do for them. After deny-
ing God's character and promises, they face his judgment—thirty-
eight more years in the wilderness.

Deuteronomy Overview

While reading Deuteronomy, you'll experience your first dose of
extended repetition in the Bible. Although it can make for tedious reading, embrace the repetition as an opportunity to order biblical events
more firmly in your mind. This book is important because it greatly
influenced Judah and Israel's prophets, who in turn influenced key New
Testament characters such as Paul and Jesus. As you read, notice the
emphasis on worshiping God and God alone. Note how often Moses

mentions that God will fulfill his promise to Abraham and give the Israelites the Promised Land.

Read This Week

Pages 84–168 of *NIV Bible in 90 Days* (Lev. 1:1–Deut. 23:11)

Personal Progress

If it is helpful to do so, use the following chart to record your reading progress during the coming week. Establish a reading schedule that works well for you and stick with it. If you are behind in your reading, set aside extra time this week to catch up.

✓	Day	Pages from the *NIV Bible in 90 Days*	Passage begins:
	1 (Today)	84–96	Leviticus 1:1
	2	96–108	Leviticus 14:33
	3	108–120	Leviticus 26:27
	4	120–132	Numbers 8:15
	5	132–144	Numbers 21:8
	6	144–156	Numbers 32:20
	7	157–168	Deuteronomy 8:1

Personal Reading Notes

Take a moment to record the highlights—knowledge gained, puzzling questions, "aha! moments"—you experience during your reading this week.

Try It!

Memorize the names of the next five books of the Bible:

Joshua   _Judges_

Ruth   1 S_amuel_

2 S_amuel_

After you've mastered the names above, try recalling all the books you've memorized thus far.

Genesis
Exodus
Leviticus
Numbers
Deuteronomy
Joshua
Judges
Ruth
1 Samuel
2 Samuel

READING OUTLINE

Discuss Today: pages 84–168 of *NIV Bible in 90 Days* (Lev. 1:1–Deut. 23:11)

Reading for the Coming Week: pages 168–252 of *NIV Bible in 90 Days* (Deut. 23:12–1 Sam. 28:19)

SMALL GROUP DISCUSSION

Reading Follow-up

1. How was your reading this week? What challenges did you face in getting your reading done? What was the most effective thing you did to meet those challenges?

2. What kind of reading routine seems to work best for you, given your activities and schedule?

3. As you read the Bible this week, which particular thought(s) and/ or event(s) stood out to you or surprised you? Why?

4. Which question(s) came up during your reading for which you'd like to find answers?

Reading Discovery

Note: The following questions are intended to stimulate discussion. There is no need to answer them prior to your class or small group meeting.

1. What important purpose and role did religious rituals — sacrifices, offerings, and feasts — play in the Israelites' lives? As you read about these practices, what insights did you gain regarding God's involvement in the lives of his people and the worship and commitment to holiness he desires?

2. Why did the people have to offer blood sacrifices?

3. Despite all that God had done for them, the Israelites repeatedly disobeyed, complained, and turned away from him. What kinds of temptations did Satan use to draw the Israelites away from God? What kinds of things did they complain about? How different are these from our temptations and complaints?

4. How did God respond to their complaints and disobedience, and what does his response reveal about him?

5. When the spies returned from scouting in Canaan, how did the people respond to their report? What did the people's words and actions reveal about their view of God?

6. As a new generation of Israelites prepared to enter the Promised Land, Moses, their 120-year-old leader, recounted the events that had taken place on their journey from Egypt and gave them a "refresher course" concerning the covenant God had made with them. What strengths and weaknesses did Moses demonstrate during these trying times in Israel's fledgling history? How do you think his words and example influenced the people?

Did You Know?

- God and his holiness are the dominant themes of Leviticus. The word *holy* appears more times in Leviticus than in any other book of the Bible. And in just nine chapters of the book, God states "I am the LORD" forty-seven times (*NIV Study Bible*, note for Lev. 18:2).

- Although the requirements for cleanliness and perfection found in the Old Testament laws may offend modern readers, it is important to remember that God is perfect and we are not. Just as Israel was required to sacrifice perfect animals in order to maintain their relationship with the holy God, we also need a perfect substitute for our sins. Jesus provided that substitute when he sacrificed himself for us on the cross.

- The same Hebrew word used for an international treaty is also used for a covenant between God and his people (*Handbook*, 210). The Sinai covenant, the most important Old Testament covenant, was the key step in Israel becoming a nation. It followed the covenant God made with Noah (Gen. 9) and the two covenants God made with Abraham (Gen. 15, 17). At Sinai, God not only gave his law to Israel, he called them to be holy and to give him exclusive allegiance: he called them as a nation into a new relationship with him (*Handbook*, 211).

VIDEO DISCUSSION (OPTIONAL)

1. As you watched the video, which particular point(s) stood out to you? Why?

2. Which aspect of the video particularly enhanced your understanding of what you read this past week?

3. What would you identify as the key themes of this portion of Scripture?

4. What impact can what you've just seen make on your life today?

This Week's Reading Tip

If you are behind in your reading, catch up by reading
on Sunday as long as necessary.

Deuteronomy Overview

In this final section of Deuteronomy, pay attention to the predictions God instructs Moses to give concerning Israel. Imagine what it would have been like to be camped on the east side of the Jordan River, poised to enter Canaan, and to hear these words from Moses. Notice the choice Joshua and Moses urged the people to make so that God would bless them with a full, productive, and meaningful life (Deut. 30:19–20; 32:44–47).

Joshua Overview

Here we see God fulfill his promises to the early patriarchs and the Israelites as they enter and settle in the Promised Land. Take note of Joshua's faithfulness to God as he leads Israel in conquering the Canaanites, which is one of the high points of Israel's history. Joshua's faithful leadership brings great reward to the nation, but even so, Israel is not entirely faithful in obeying God's commands.

Judges Overview

Here you'll see how quickly Israel forgets about God and rejects his kingship. Note the strengths and weaknesses of the various judges — including Deborah, Gideon, and Samson — whom God sent to assist Israel during critical times. Consider also the cycle that begins during this time period: Israel breaks its covenant with God, God sends foreign oppressors to punish his people, they cry out for help, he faithfully delivers them, and then they disobey again.

Ruth Overview

In many ways the book of Ruth portrays the promise of a life far beyond one's expectations. As you read this book, which reads like a short story, take note of the themes of faithful love and redemption that prevail as events unfold for an Israelite family.

1 Samuel Overview

The events of 1 Samuel take place during a time of political, social, and spiritual turmoil. Observe how Israel refuses to listen to God and makes the rough transition from the time of the judges to the reign of Saul, Israel's first earthly king. Notice the ups and downs David, the great warrior, faces before he becomes Israel's next king.

Read This Week

Pages 168–252 of *NIV Bible in 90 Days* (Deut. 23:12–1 Sam. 28:19)

Personal Progress

If it is helpful to do so, use the following chart to record your reading progress this week. Establish a reading schedule that works well for you—then stick with it.

✓	Day	Pages from the *NIV Bible in 90 Days*	Passage begins:
	1 (Today)	168–180	Deuteronomy 23:12
	2	180–192	Joshua 1:1
	3	192–204	Joshua 15:1
	4	205–216	Judges 3:28
	5	216–228	Judges 15:13
	6	228–240	1 Samuel 2:30
	7	240–252	1 Samuel 16:1

If you are behind in your reading, set aside extra time this week to catch up.

Personal Reading Notes

Take a moment to record the highlights—knowledge gained, puzzling questions, "aha! moments"—you experience during your reading this week.

Try It!

Memorize the names of the next five books of the Bible:

1 K_____   2 K_____

1 C_____   2 C_____

E_____

After you've mastered the names above, try recalling all the books you've memorized thus far.

READING OUTLINE

Discuss Today: pages 168–252 of *NIV Bible in 90 Days* (Deut. 23:12–1 Sam. 28:19)

Reading for the Coming Week: pages 252–336 of *NIV Bible in 90 Days* (1 Sam 28:20–2 Kings 25:30)

SMALL GROUP DISCUSSION

Reading Follow-up

1. How was your reading this week? What challenges did you face in getting your reading done? What was the most effective thing you did to meet those challenges?

2. As you read the Bible this week, which particular thought(s) and/ or event(s) stood out to you or surprised you? Why?

3. Which question(s) came up during your reading for which you'd like to find answers?

4. In what ways is your reading affecting your view of God, his Word, and your relationship with him?

Reading Discovery

Note: The following questions are intended to stimulate discussion. There is no need to answer them prior to your class or small group meeting.

1. Although God lived among the Israelites and guided them in battle, the Gibeonites still were able to deceive Joshua and other leaders. How did this happen? (See Josh. 9.)

2. What was God's intent in repeatedly commanding the Israelites to destroy the Canaanites? Why was God so harsh in dealing with paganism? What does this reveal about God and his view of sin?

3. To what extent had the people of Israel assimilated into the Canaanite culture by the end of the book of Judges? In what ways does Samson's life illustrate the effects of sin? What does Samson's life reveal about the unlikely people and events through which God sometimes works?

4. What tragedies and unfortunate events befell Naomi and Ruth? What themes surfaced as these events played out in their story?

5. When the Israelites asked Samuel to appoint a king, what were they communicating about God and his kingship over them? (See 1 Sam. 8.)

6. As you read about David's life following his anointing and before he became king, what did you learn about him that you hadn't realized before? What kind of a man was he?

Did You Know?

- The Israelites entered Canaan, the territory we know as the coast of modern Lebanon and Israel, in about 1250 BC during what biblical archaeologists call the Late Bronze Age (*NIV Study Bible*, 289). Although none of the powerful nations of the ancient Near East — Egypt, Babylon, Assyria — had a strong presence in Canaan at that time, the Canaanites were extensive traders. Thousands of artifacts unearthed in ancient sites reveal that Canaanite culture was quite advanced — in many ways superior to that of Israel (*Handbook, 231*).

- Just how much trouble had Samson caused for the Philistines? Consider this: In order to entice Delilah to trap Samson, each of the five Philistine rulers offered her 1,100 shekels of silver — a sum that was equivalent to the price of 275 slaves (*NIV Study Bible*, note on Judg. 16:5).

- Moab, where Ruth grew up, was located east of the Dead Sea and west of the desert along both sides of the Arnon River gorge (*NIV Study Bible*, 366). Descendants of Lot's first son, Moab, these people did everything they could to block Israel's expansion. The king of Moab hired the prophet Balaam to curse Israel (Num. 22 – 24); Moabite women drew Israelite men into immorality (Num. 25). Later, Chemosh, the Moabites' primary god, proved to be a strong lure. Even King Solomon built a sacred site for Chemosh worship on a hill east of Jerusalem, which resulted in God's judgment and the divided kingdoms of Israel and Judah (1 Kings 11:10 – 13).

VIDEO DISCUSSION (OPTIONAL)

1. As you watched the video, which particular point(s) stood out to you? Why?

2. Which aspect of the video particularly enhanced your understanding of what you read this past week?

3. What would you identify as the key themes of this portion of Scripture?

4. What impact can what you've just seen make on your life today?

This Week's Reading Tip

Remember your mission: "To read *attentively* every word of the Bible in 90 days."

2 Samuel Overview

A record of David's reign as king through his old age, 2 Samuel depicts the most magnificent high points as well as the low points of David's life and that of his family. David's affair with Bathsheba—an ugly story of lust, abuse of power, deceit, and murder—is but a preview of what follows. In fulfillment of Nathan's prophecy that David's sin with Bathsheba would split the house of David, we see the consequences unfold, bringing division and suffering not only to David's family but to the entire nation of Israel.

1 Kings Overview

First Kings picks up where 2 Samuel left off. After Solomon's death, watch for the brutal causes and results as Israel splits into two kingdoms. It can be challenging to keep it all straight, but you will see a succession of kings of both kingdoms. Pay attention to which kings of Israel (north) and Judah (south) do "right in the eyes of the LORD" and which ones don't. Notice how God responds.

2 Kings Overview

As you read the continuing story of the two kingdoms, imagine what it was like for God's people who repeatedly compromised with evil until they faced God's judgment. Notice how the prophets Elijah and Elisha respond as they try to guide the people toward God. Watch for the destruction of Jerusalem, which is the climax of the Old Testament's plot.

Read This Week

Pages 252–336 of *NIV Bible in 90 Days* (1 Sam. 28:20–2 Kings 25:30)

Personal Progress

If it is helpful to do so, use the following chart to record your reading progress this week. Establish a reading schedule that works well for you—then stick with it.

✓	Day	Pages from the *NIV Bible in 90 Days*	Passage begins:
	1 (Today)	252–264	1 Samuel 28:20
	2	264–276	2 Samuel 12:11
	3	277–288	2 Samuel 22:19
	4	288–300	1 Kings 7:38
	5	300–312	1 Kings 16:21
	6	312–324	2 Kings 4:38
	7	324–336	2 Kings 15:27

If you are behind in your reading, set aside extra time this week to catch up.

Personal Reading Notes

Take a moment to record the highlights—knowledge gained, puzzling questions, "aha! moments"—you experience during your reading this week.

Try It!

Memorize the names of the next five books of the Bible:

N_____ E_____

J_____ P_____

P_____

After you've mastered the names above, try recalling all the books you've memorized thus far.

READING OUTLINE

Discuss Today: pages 252 – 336 of *NIV Bible in 90 Days*
(1 Sam. 28:20 – 2 Kings 25:30)

Reading for the Coming Week: pages 336 – 420 of *NIV Bible in 90 Days* (1 Chron. 1:1 – Neh. 13:14)

SMALL GROUP DISCUSSION

Reading Follow-up

1. How was your reading this week? What challenges did you face in getting your reading done? What was the most effective thing you did to meet those challenges?

2. As you read the Bible this week, which particular thought(s) and/ or event(s) stood out to you or surprised you? Why?

3. Which question(s) came up during your reading for which you'd like to find answers?

4. In what ways is your reading affecting your view of God, his Word, and your relationship with him?

Reading Discovery

Note: The following questions are intended to stimulate discussion. There is no need to answer them prior to your class or small group meeting.

1. What important promise did God make to David concerning the future of his dynasty? (See 2 Sam. 7:11b, 16.)

2. Which character weaknesses and failures played a dramatic role in David's life? What was God's response when David publicly acknowledged his sins and asked for God's forgiveness? In what ways did the consequences of David's extramarital affair affect his family and, eventually, the entire nation?

3. How would you describe Solomon? What do you find admirable (and not so admirable) about him? What drew him away from God? Why did the people eventually rebel against him?

4. What factors caused the nation of Israel to split into the northern kingdom (Israel) and the southern kingdom (Judah)?

5. When you consider the bravery of Elijah and Elisha in opposing idol worship in the northern kingdom of Israel, what stands out to you concerning their relationship with God and/or the people? Why?

6. What would you identify as the dominant tendency of the various kings who led Israel and Judah? In what ways did they disobey God? What distinguished King Josiah from many other kings? (See 2 Kings 22–23.)

Did You Know?

- After the kingdom of Israel split, none of the nineteen kings of Israel did what was right in the eyes of God. So God allowed Assyria to defeat Israel in 722 BC, and the scattered survivors disappear from recorded history. Of the nineteen kings of Judah, only a handful worked to guide the people toward God, so God allowed the Babylonians to destroy Judah and take its people to Babylon.

- Jerusalem, the city King David established as his royal city and Israel's capital, was first populated during the third millenium BC. The fortresslike city sat on a hill with deep valleys on three sides and received water from an underground source (*NIV Study Bible*, 431). The tribes of Judah and Benjamin attacked the city during the conquest of Canaan and set the city on fire, but the Jebusites later recaptured it (Josh. 15:63). The Israelites didn't control Jerusalem until about 1000 BC, when David captured it by entering through a tunnel that brought water into the city (*Handbook*, 267). At that time, the city was quite small — smaller than eleven acres in size with no more than 3,500 people. Strategically located on the border of Israel and Judah, Jerusalem's location helped David unite both kingdoms without showing favor to either one (*NIV Study Bible*, note on 2 Sam. 5:6).

- God promised to establish David's "house" — a royal dynasty — that would last forever (2 Sam. 7:11 – 16). Ultimately, God fulfilled his covenant with David through the kingship of Jesus Christ, who was born of the house of David of the tribe of Judah (*NIV Study Bible*, note on 2 Sam. 7:11).

VIDEO DISCUSSION (OPTIONAL)

1. As you watched the video, which particular point(s) stood out to you? Why?

2. Which aspect of the video particularly enhanced your understanding of what you read this past week?

3. What would you identify as the key themes of this portion of Scripture?

4. What impact can what you've just seen make on your life today?

This Week's Reading Tip

If you need a little variation, try reading at a different time
of day or in a different place.

1 Chronicles Overview

Written for the exiles who had returned to rebuild Jerusalem under
Ezra and Nehemiah, 1 Chronicles traces the genealogy and inter-
prets the history of God's people (primarily from 1–2 Samuel and
1–2 Kings). You will notice an emphasis on the political and spiritual
events of David's reign and the covenant promises God was keeping by
establishing David as Israel's king.

2 Chronicles Overview

This book records the deeds of all the kings of Judah who came after
Solomon. Pay attention to how often the phrases "was fully committed
to the Lord" (15:17) or "did evil in the eyes of the Lord" (21:6) appear
because they illustrate what really matters to God (and should matter
to us as well).

Ezra Overview

Both Ezra and Nehemiah tell about the rebuilding of Jerusalem.
Notice how God uses Ezra—a priest and scribe—to restore Israel's
identity among the Jewish exiles. He challenges the people—who have
spent decades in Persian society disregarding God's law and mixing
worship of the God of the covenant with worship of foreign gods—to
fully uphold God's law.

Nehemiah Overview

In this book you'll see how God used Nehemiah's prayers, plans,
and passion to accomplish great things. He not only led the people in
rebuilding the wall around Jerusalem, he helped restore Jewish tradi-
tion and faithfulness to God in the community.

Read This Week

Pages 336–420 of *NIV Bible in 90 Days* (1 Chron. 1:1–Neh. 13:14)

Personal Progress

If it is helpful to do so, use the following chart to record your reading progress this week. Establish a reading schedule that works well for you—then stick with it.

✓	Day	Pages from the *NIV Bible in 90 Days*	Passage begins:
	1 (Today)	336–348	1 Chronicles 1:1
	2	349–360	1 Chronicles 10:1
	3	360–372	1 Chronicles 24:1
	4	372–384	2 Chronicles 7:11
	5	384–396	2 Chronicles 23:16
	6	396–408	2 Chronicles 35:16
	7	408–420	Nehemiah 1:1

If you are behind in your reading, set aside extra time this week to catch up.

Personal Reading Notes

Take a moment to record the highlights—knowledge gained, puzzling questions, "aha! moments"—you experience during your reading this week.

Try It!

Memorize the names of the next five books of the Bible:

E_____   S_____

I_____   J_____

L_____

After you've mastered the names above, try recalling all the books you've memorized thus far.

READING OUTLINE

Discuss Today: pages 336 – 420 of *NIV Bible in 90 Days*
(1 Chron. 1:1 – Neh. 13:14)

Reading for the Coming Week: pages 420 – 504 of *NIV Bible
in 90 Days* (Neh. 13:15 – Ps. 89:13)

SMALL GROUP DISCUSSIONS

Reading Follow-up

1. How was your reading this week? What challenges did you face in getting your reading done? What was the most effective thing you did to meet those challenges?

2. As you read the Bible this week, which particular thought(s) and/ or event(s) stood out to you or surprised you? Why?

3. Which question(s) came up during your reading for which you'd like to find answers?

4. In what ways is your reading affecting your view of God, his Word, and your relationship with him?

Reading Discovery

Note: The following questions are intended to stimulate discussion. There is no need to answer them prior to your class or small group meeting.

1. Imagine that you were an exile returning to Jerusalem. What in 1 Chronicles would you have found inspiring about Israel's history and God's promises concerning David's dynasty? About the need to remain faithful to God?

2. Which themes did you notice in David's prayer shortly before his death (1 Chron. 29) and Solomon's prayer at the temple's dedication (2 Chron. 6)?

3. As you read 2 Chronicles, what did you notice about the activities of the kings of Judah?

4. Describe Ezra and the challenges he faced when he returned to Jerusalem from Babylon. How did the people respond when Ezra helped them finally know God's standards and recognize their own wrongdoing? Why was it so important for them to confess their sins and follow God's law?

5. Why was ethnic purity so vital to the nation's existence? (See Ezra 10 and Neh. 9.)

6. Where did Nehemiah's loyalties lie? In what ways did he demonstrate his reliance on God and deep commitment to prayer as he accomplished a great work in what the Persians considered to be a rebellious city?

Did You Know?

- The readings this week have been a kind of epilogue to the fall of Jerusalem, which is the climactic point of Old Testament history. The book of Nehemiah, although it is not the end of the Old Testament, covers the final events in Old Testament history. The remaining books of the Old Testament either fill in information along the previous timeline or provide an artistic, philosophical, or prophetic view of events about which, for the most part, you have already read.

- Ezra took on an unpopular issue when he spoke out against mixed marriages between God's people and heathen people. God forbade such marriages because they led to idolatry, yet even priests, kings, and Levites had done it. Some of the men (see Mal. 2:10 – 16) had even broken marriages to Jewish wives in order to marry idol-worshiping women.

- To reach Jerusalem from the Persians' winter capital of Susa, about two hundred miles east of Babylon, Nehemiah traveled about 1,100 miles — quite a distance even today (*Handbook*, 334, 340).

VIDEO DISCUSSION (OPTIONAL)

1. As you watched the video, which particular point(s) stood out to you? Why?

2. Which aspect of the video particularly enhanced your understanding of what you read this past week?

3. What would you identify as the key themes of this portion of Scripture?

4. What impact can what you've just seen make on your life today?

This Week's Reading Tip

Remember, don't get bogged down trying to understand everything you read. Press on and pay attention to what you do understand.

Esther Overview

As you read the story of Esther, try putting yourself in her position. Watch her faith in God grow, and notice how God uses her courageous actions and those of Mordecai to save the Jews from annihilation. Consider, too, that Esther lived in Persia about thirty years before the events recorded in Nehemiah. How might her actions have affected what occurred during Nehemiah's time?

Job Overview

Pay close attention to the scenario set up in this book, which probably took place during the time of Abraham, Isaac, and Jacob. As you read, reflect on the insights into the nature of suffering and faith, who God is and how deeply he values righteousness, and the unseen spiritual conflicts between God's kingdom and Satan's kingdom.

Psalms Overview

While reading the poetic prayers and hymns in this book, note those that especially connect with you. You'll want to return to them for further reading at a later date. Pay close attention to what the psalms reveal about faith, godliness, hope, justice, and God being at the center of life.

Read This Week

Pages 420–504 of *NIV Bible in 90 Days* (Neh. 13:15–Ps. 89:13)

Personal Progress

If it is helpful to do so, use the following chart to record your reading progress this week. Establish a reading schedule that works well for you—then stick with it.

✓	Day	Pages in the *NIV Bible in 90 Days*	Passage begins:
	1 (Today)	420–433	Nehemiah 13:15
	2	433–444	Job 8:1
	3	444–456	Job 25:1
	4	456–468	Job 42:1
	5	468–480	Psalm 25:1
	6	480–492	Psalm 45:15
	7	492–504	Psalm 69:22

If you are behind in your reading, set aside extra time this week to catch up.

Personal Reading Notes

Take a moment to record highlights—knowledge gained, puzzling questions, "aha! moments"—you experience during your reading this week.

Try It!

Memorize the names of the next five books of the Bible:

E_____   D_____

H_____   J_____

A_____

After you've mastered the names above, try recalling all the books you've memorized thus far.

READING OUTLINE

Discuss Today: pages 420–504 of *NIV Bible in 90 Days* (Neh. 13:15–Ps. 89:13)

Reading for the Coming Week: pages 504–588 of *NIV Bible in 90 Days* (Ps. 89:14–Isa. 13:22)

SMALL GROUP DISCUSSION

Reading Follow-up

1. How was your reading this week? What new challenges are you facing in accomplishing your reading? What was the most effective thing you did to meet those challenges?

2. As you read the Bible this week, which particular thought(s) and/ or event(s) stood out to you or surprised you? Why?

3. Which question(s) came up during your reading for which you'd like to find answers?

4. In what ways is your reading affecting your view of God, his Word, and your relationship with him?

Reading Discovery

Note: The following questions are intended to stimulate discussion. There is no need to answer them prior to your class or small group meeting.

1. Since the word *God* never appears in the book of Esther, why do you think this book is included in the Bible?

2. What does Esther's story reveal to you about faith and trust in God and the relationship between human responsibility and divine sovereignty?

3. Many people view Job as a book about suffering and patience. Build a case for the contention that the book is really about faith.

4. How did God answer Job's questions? In what ways does God's response to Job answer the difficult questions in your life? How satisfactory is that response to you?

5. Which psalm(s) that you read this week particularly connected with you? Why?

6. In what ways did this week's readings impact your thinking on a current event or personal experience?

Did You Know?

- God commanded King Saul to execute the Amalekites and their evil king Agag because the Amalekites were the first people to attack the Israelites after their departure from Egypt (Ex. 17:8 – 16; 1 Sam. 15:2). But Saul disobeyed God and spared Agag. As it turns out, Haman probably was a descendant of Agag (Est. 3:1)! Using Haman, Satan again tried to destroy God's people and his unfolding plans. At stake was not only the Jews' existence but the future appearance of Jesus, the Messiah.

- In his defense, Job referred to his time as a healthy man (ch. 29) when he took his seat at "the gate of the city." This means that Job had been an influential leader in his community. During ancient times, the city elders presided over the most important legal cases and administrative business at the city gate – the equivalent of what we would call "city hall" (*NIV Study Bible,* notes for Job 29:7; Ruth 4:1; Gen. 19:1).

- The book of Psalms was collected during a six-hundred-year period from the time of David to the time of Ezra (*You Are Here in the Bible*, Psalms). Written as many as a thousand years before Jesus' birth, some psalms clearly point to the coming Messiah (see Pss. 2, 8, 16, 22, 69, 72, 89, 110, 118, 132). The prophetic nature of the psalms is validated by the New Testament, which references at least seventeen instances where the book of Psalms refers to Christ.

VIDEO DISCUSSION (OPTIONAL)

1. As you watched the video, which particular point(s) stood out to you? Why?

2. Which aspect of the video particularly enhanced your understanding of what you read this past week?

3. What would you identify as the key themes of this portion of Scripture?

4. What impact can what you've just seen make on your life today?

This Week's Reading Tip

Read *attentively* and build on the broad overview of Bible history you are gaining through your reading.

Psalms Overview

Continue to note the particular psalms that especially connect with you. Consider the many ways the psalmists praise God for who he is and what he has done. Take note of references in the psalms to events about which you already have read (Israel's time in the wilderness described in Ps. 95:10, for example).

Proverbs Overview

As you read this book of short sayings that illustrate general principles for making wise choices in life, notice the repetition of various themes—family relationships, fruitful labor, fidelity, reverence for and trust in the Creator God, ways and consequences of folly, responsibilities, and so on. Compare what Proverbs says about wisdom to what many people today would say about it.

Ecclesiastes Overview

As you ponder this exploration into the meaning and futility of life, don't miss the subtle theme that somehow—despite the confusion, uncertainty, and pain—there is a God who has placed eternity in our hearts, who desires our love and reverence, who offers us hope in himself. Although much of the book expresses the futility of a life lived without God, notice the book's concluding statement of hope.

Song of Songs Overview

This book's celebration of love is often interpreted in several ways—as an allegory, wisdom literature, a love song, or a combination thereof. As you read, reflect on the images of sexual love, marital fidelity, and the couple's shameless enjoyment of their God-given sexuality.

Isaiah Overview

Notice the strong themes of destruction and redemption that occur within the context of the spiritual turmoil of Judah and other nations. (Don't be overly concerned about hard-to-understand visions and prophecies.) Watch for allusions to events you have already read about, such as Sodom and Gomorrah (Isa. 1:9).

Read This Week

Pages 504–588 of *NIV Bible in 90 Days* (Ps. 89:14–Isa. 13:22)

Personal Progress

If it is helpful to do so, use the following chart to record your reading progress this week. Establish a reading schedule that works well for you—then stick with it.

✓	Day	Pages in the *NIV Bible in 90 Days*	Passage begins:
	1 (Today)	504–517	Psalm 89:14
	2	517–528	Psalm 109:1
	3	528–540	Psalm 135:1
	4	540–552	Proverbs 7:1
	5	552–564	Proverbs 20:22
	6	564–576	Ecclesiastes 3:1
	7	577–588	Isaiah 1:1

If you are behind in your reading, set aside extra time this week to catch up.

Personal Reading Notes

Take a moment to record the highlights—knowledge gained, puzzling questions, "aha! moments"—you experience during your reading this week.

Try It!

Memorize the names of the next five books of the Bible:

O_____   J_____

M_____   N_____

H_____

After you've mastered the names above, try recalling all the books you've memorized thus far.

READING OUTLINE

Discuss Today: pages 504 – 588 of *NIV Bible in 90 Days* (Ps.
89:14 – Isa. 13:22)

Reading for the Coming Week: pages 588 – 672 of *NIV Bible in 90
Days* (Isa. 14:1 – Jer. 33:22)

SMALL GROUP DISCUSSION

Reading Follow-up

1. How was your reading this week? What new challenges did you
   face in accomplishing your reading? What was the most effective
   thing you did to meet those challenges?

2. As you read the Bible this week, which particular thought(s) and/
   or event(s) stood out to you or surprised you? Why?

3. Which question(s) came up during your reading for which you'd like to find answers?

4. In what ways is your reading affecting your view of God, his Word, and your relationship with him?

Reading Discovery

Note: The following questions are intended to stimulate discussion. There is no need to answer them prior to your class or small group meeting.

1. Many of the psalms in this week's reading were psalms of thanksgiving and praise to God for who he is and what he has done. In what new ways can you praise and thank God as a result of your reading?

2. Although the book of Proverbs offers abundant wisdom for making choices that usually yield more desirable outcomes in life, why is it important to remember that God doesn't *guarantee* particular outcomes if we adopt these general principles?

3. What is your favorite proverb, and why is it meaningful to you? What changes might occur in the world if more people practiced the general principle expressed in that proverb?

4. In what ways was your perspective on life challenged or changed as you read Ecclesiastes? What do you believe is the foundation of true wisdom and a meaningful life?

5. Ecclesiastes and Song of Songs are both attributed to Solomon, but they are very different books. The dominant spirit of Ecclesiastes could be described in three questions: What can I get? Where can I find pleasure? What will life do for me? In contrast, how would you describe the spirit of Song of Songs?

6. Song of Songs has been interpreted many ways including: (1) an allegory describing God's love, (2) wisdom literature describing an ideal relationship between a husband and his wife, (3) a love song from Solomon to a peasant girl (perhaps his first wife), or (4) a combination of the above. What do you think it is?

Did You Know?

- Psalm 114, the "Passover hymn," celebrates the exodus and probably was composed after Israel and Judah divided. It was likely written for liturgical use at the temple during a religious festival. Scholars consider this hymn to be one of the best-fashioned songs of the Psalter (*NIV Study Bible*, note for Ps. 114).

- Vivid images from everyday life are frequently used to communicate the principles presented in the book of Proverbs. Consider, for example: (1) Rubies, which were the most priceless jewels in the ancient world. Proverbs 3:15 compares wisdom to rubies and Proverbs 31:10 compares the wife of noble character to rubies. (2) The "colored linens from Egypt" (Prov. 7:16). Egyptian linen was expensive, so it is associated with wealth. (3) Silver was weighed on scales (Prov. 11:1), balanced against a specific stone weight. Dishonest people improperly labeled their weights (*NIV Study Bible*, verse notes).

- The "sachet of myrrh" mentioned in Song of Songs 1:13 was an aromatic gum derived from balsam trees in India, Ethiopia, and Arabia. Used as a perfume, this gum was also an ingredient in holy anointing oil. The wise men brought myrrh to Jesus as a gift (Matt. 2:2, 11).

VIDEO DISCUSSION (OPTIONAL)

1. As you watched the video, which particular point(s) stood out to you? Why?

2. Which aspect of the video particularly enhanced your understanding of what you read this past week?

3. What would you identify as the key themes of this portion of Scripture?

4. What impact can what you've just seen make on your life today?

This Week's Reading Tip

When reading the books of the prophets, it is helpful to remember *to whom* the prophet is writing, *when* the prophet is writing, and the *circumstances* of the prophet's audience.

Isaiah Overview

The strong warnings of destruction continue, but as the book progresses you will discover a message of comfort, encouragement, and a future hope. Pay attention to the praise Isaiah offers to God, the beautiful poetry in chapters 36–39, and the powerful imagery Isaiah uses.

Jeremiah Overview

Imagine what it must have been like to rail against the sin of God's people for forty years! While Jeremiah was not popular among his contemporaries, he is the prophet Jesus most often quoted. As you read, notice how often Jeremiah warns the kingdom of Judah to stop committing adultery, using perverted worship practices, and in general turning away from God. Notice how the people respond to Jeremiah as he keeps to his mission and the hard questions Jeremiah keeps asking.

Read This Week

Pages 588–672 of *NIV Bible in 90 Days* (Isa. 14:1–Jer. 33:22)

Personal Progress

If it is helpful to do so, use the following chart to record your reading progress this week. Establish a reading schedule that works well for you—then stick with it.

✓	Day	Pages in the *NIV Bible in 90 Days*	Passage begins:
	1 (Today)	588–600	Isaiah 14:1
	2	600–612	Isaiah 29:1
	3	612–624	Isaiah 41:19
	4	624–636	Isaiah 52:13
	5	636–648	Isaiah 66:19
	6	648–660	Jeremiah 10:14
	7	660–672	Jeremiah 23:9

If you are behind in your reading, set aside extra time this week to catch up.

Personal Reading Notes

Take a moment to record the highlights—knowledge gained, puzzling questions, "aha! moments"—you experience during your reading this week.

Try It!

Memorize the names of the final four books of the Old Testament:

Z_____   H_____

Z_____   M_____

After you've mastered the names above, try recalling all the books you've memorized thus far.

READING OUTLINE

Discuss Today: pages 588 – 672 of *NIV Bible in 90 Days* (Isa. 14:1 –
Jer. 33:22)

Reading for the Coming Week: pages 672 – 756 of *NIV Bible in 90 Days*
(Jer. 33:23 – Dan. 8:27)

SMALL GROUP DISCUSSION

Reading Follow-up

1. How was your reading this week? What new challenges did you
   face in accomplishing your reading? What was the most effective
   thing you did to meet those challenges?

2. As you read the Bible this week, which particular thought(s) and/
   or event(s) stood out to you or surprised you? Why?

3. Which question(s) came up during your reading for which you'd like to find answers?

4. In what ways is your reading affecting your view of God, his Word, and your relationship with him?

Reading Discovery

Note: The following questions are intended to stimulate discussion. There is no need to answer them prior to your class or small group meeting.

1. What do you think are the major themes and incidents recorded in Isaiah? And in Jeremiah?

2. God's awesome holiness, our unrighteousness and need for purification, and God's promise of redemption and restoration are key themes of God's call on Isaiah's life (Isa. 6). In what ways are these themes evident throughout the book of Isaiah?

3. Read aloud some of the prophetic passages in the book of Isaiah concerning the coming Messiah. What do these passages reveal about him and the hope in store for God's people?

4. Both Isaiah and Jeremiah served as God's advocates before ungodly kings of Judah. How did each prophet feel about the responsibility God had given? How would you feel if you were assigned to be a similar type of advocate for God today?

5. What common image from daily life did God use to communicate his message to Jeremiah, and what common object from daily life did Jeremiah use to communicate God's message to the people (Jer. 18–20)? How effective was Jeremiah's communication? What was the result?

6. In what way(s) did this week's readings impact your thoughts on a current event or personal experience?

Did You Know?

- The Old Testament prophet's primary role was not to give people a glimpse of a blueprint of future events, but to encourage people to live now in the way that God wanted, a way that reflected the fact of their relationship to him. Prophets were responsible to speak out clearly the things God had given them to say. However, listeners had responsibilities too. They were, of course, responsible to hear and heed the things said to them; to turn their faith into action; to live out the justice and holiness and love of their God. They were also responsible for assessing whether or not the prophet was really speaking from God, responsible for being honest with themselves and with God and in particular for not trying to bribe the prophet to give nice warm messages that only ever contained the things they wanted to hear (Isa. 30:10 – 11; Jer. 5:31). (See *Handbook*, 423 – 424.)

- Some of Isaiah's prophecies related to imminent events, not just distant events. For example, in Isaiah 10:24 – 27, he predicted that God would annihilate the Assyrian army. This occurred in 701 BC (*NIV Study Bible*, note for Isa. 9:4).

- At the time Isaiah prophesied against the city of Babylon, its beautiful temples and palaces were world renowned. In fact, the hanging gardens of King Nebuchadnezzar (605 – 562 BC) were one of the seven wonders of the ancient world (*NIV Study Bible*, note for Isa. 13:19). In addition, the city boasted incredible canals, numerous monuments, a staged temple tower 295 feet high, and city walls wide enough that a four-horse chariot could turn around on top of them (*NIV Study Bible*, 1325). The Babylonians brought about the downfall of Jerusalem and Judah between 605 and 586 BC, but Cyrus the Persian conquered Babylon in 539 BC (*NIV Study Bible*, note for Isa. 13:1). Persian King Xerxes almost completely destroyed Babylon in 478 BC, and after the time of Alexander the Great in 330 BC, Babylon fell into complete disrepair and has remained that way (*NIV Study Bible*, note for Isa. 13:20). Revelation 18:2 describes ruined Babylon as a home for demons and evil spirits.

VIDEO DISCUSSION (OPTIONAL)

1. As you watched the video, which particular point(s) stood out to you? Why?

2. Which aspect of the video particularly enhanced your understanding of what you read this past week?

3. What would you identify as the key themes of this portion of Scripture?

4. What impact can what you've just seen make on your life today?

This Week's Reading Tip

Remember, don't expect to understand everything you read.
Pay attention to what you do understand,
and don't worry about the rest.

Jeremiah Overview

Jeremiah's persecution and suffering increases as God's judgment approaches; he is actually in chains when the Babylonians take over Jerusalem. Take special notice of Jeremiah's ongoing role as God's messenger to the remnant of Judah that is not taken away to Babylon. Consider what happens to them and how God responds to the nations that have battled his people.

Lamentations Overview

As you read this poetic book of laments over Jerusalem's destruction in 586 BC and descriptions of devastation and slaughter, try to imagine the Jews' deep loss. Not only have their city and temple been destroyed, they have been exiled from the homeland God had given them. Although God ordained their punishment, notice the hope, love, faithfulness, and salvation he continues to offer.

Ezekiel Overview

Although parts of Ezekiel can be difficult to understand, pay attention to the constant theme that God is sovereign over nations, people, history, and all creation. As you read, consider why God repeats variations of: "Then they will know that I am the LORD." Notice, too, the theme of holiness and what Ezekiel predicts concerning God's design of redemption that will unfold in the New Testament.

Daniel Overview

From the first pages of this book, Daniel stands out as a leader — spiritually and politically. Take note of the qualities of Daniel's relationship with God: his faithfulness, his faith in God, and his commitment to prayer. Consider also the repeating theme of God's sovereignty over all people (Dan. 4:17; 5:21).

Read This Week

Pages 672–756 of *NIV Bible in 90 Days* (Jer. *33:23*–Dan. 8:27)

Personal Progress

If it is helpful to do so, use the following chart to record your reading progress this week. Establish a reading schedule that works well for you—then stick with it.

✓	Day	Pages in the *NIV Bible in 90 Days*	Passage begins:
	1 (Today)	672–684	Jeremiah 33:23
	2	684–696	Jeremiah 48:1
	3	696–708	Lamentations 2:1
	4	708–720	Ezekiel 12:21
	5	720–732	Ezekiel 23:40
	6	733–744	Ezekiel 36:1
	7	745–756	Ezekiel 47:13

If you are behind in your reading, set aside extra time this week to catch up.

Personal Reading Notes

Take a moment to record the highlights—knowledge gained, puzzling questions, "aha! moments"—you experience during your reading this week.

Try It!

Review the names of the thirty-nine books of the Old Testament.

G_____   E_____

L_____   N_____

D_____   J_____

J_____   R_____

1 S_____   2 S_____

1 K_____   2 K_____

1 C_____   2 C_____

E_____   N_____

E_____   J_____

P_____   P_____

E_____   S_____

I_____   J_____

L_____   E_____

D_____   H_____

J_____   A_____

O_____   J_____

M_____   N_____

H_____   Z_____

H_____   Z_____

M_____

READING OUTLINE

Discuss Today: pages 672 – 756 of *NIV Bible in 90 Days* (Jer. 33:23 – Dan. 8:27)

Reading for the Coming Week: pages 756 – 840 of *NIV Bible in 90 Days* (Dan. 9:1 – Matt. 26:56)

SMALL GROUP DISCUSSION

Reading Follow-up

1. How was your reading this week? What new challenges did you face in accomplishing your reading? What was the most effective thing you did to meet those challenges?

2. As you read the Bible this week, which particular thought(s) and/ or event(s) stood out to you or surprised you? Why?

3. Which question(s) came up during your reading for which you'd like to find answers?

4. In what ways is your reading affecting your view of God, his Word, and your relationship with him?

Reading Discovery

Note: The following questions are intended to stimulate discussion. There is no need to answer them prior to your class or small group meeting.

1. In what ways did Jeremiah suffer as a result of his prophetic calling from God? What new things did you learn from this week's reading about the fall of Jerusalem and the fate of the tribe of Judah?

2. What were your thoughts and feelings as you read Lamentations? Which images stood out to you? Which themes surfaced related to the character of God? (See Lam. 3.)

3. Which major theme(s) occur throughout the book of Ezekiel? Why were these themes so important for God's people to understand?

4. Ezekiel is known for being a highly visual book. The prophet had some strange visions from God, and he often used strong—even shocking—visual images to communicate God's message to the people. What were some of those images, and what did they mean?

5. Which of Daniel's personal characteristics stood out to you? Why? In what ways did Daniel put his faith in God into action? What can we learn from his example about faithfully following and serving God in a hostile culture?

6. What does Daniel's interpretation of King Nebuchadnezzar's dream (Dan. 2) reveal about God's presence and involvement in the world? Why would this have been important to his original audience, the Jews living as exiles in Babylon?

Did You Know?

- The phrase "son of man" is used ninety-three times (*NIV Study Bible*, note for Ezek. 2:1) in the book of Ezekiel to emphasize Ezekiel's humanity, but the phrase is used as a proper title only in the book of Daniel. In Daniel's vision (Dan. 7:13 – 14), he saw the son of man as a heavenly figure whom God entrusts with glory, authority, and sovereign power during the end times and whose kingdom will last forever. A few centuries later Jesus used this term eighty-one times (*NIV Study Bible*, note for Mark 8:31) to describe himself, thus showing that he was the eschatological figure of whom Daniel spoke.

- Although he exiled them from their Promised Land because of their long-term disobedience, God never abandoned his covenant people. Interestingly, God continued to call his exiled people by the name "Israel" — their covenant name (Ezek. 2:3; 3:4 – 5:7; see *NIV Study Bible*, note for Ezek. 2:1 – 3:15). Even during their captivity, he continued to unfold his redemptive plan.

- Old Testament prophets often used the term *prostitution* to describe God's disobedient people. But the usage doesn't refer only to the act of sexual prostitution or even idolatry. Sometimes it refers to Israel's alliances with pagan nations and preoccupation with worldly politics, such as placing confidence in their own skills and ability to find security rather than completely relying on God (*NIV Study Bible*, note for Ezek. 23:5).

VIDEO DISCUSSION (OPTIONAL)

1. As you watched the video, which particular point(s) stood out to you? Why?

2. Which aspect of the video particularly enhanced your understanding of what you read this past week?

3. What would you identify as the key themes of this portion of Scripture?

4. What impact can what you've just seen make on your life today?

This Week's Reading Tip

As you read, remember to keep in mind *to whom* the prophet is writing, *when* the prophet is writing, and the *circumstances* of the prophet's audience. See "The Prophets in Their Place" on pages 105–106.

The Prophets in Their Place

Book	Era	Audience	Theme(s)
Isaiah (chs. 1–39)	Pre-exile c. 700 BC?	Judah	Judgment against Judah and Israel; prophecies of promise and blessing; judgments against nations.
Isaiah (chs. 40–55)	Exile c. 680 BC?	Judah	Deliverance and restoration of Israel; the servant's ministry; God's call to salvation.
Isaiah (chs. 56–66)	Uncertain	Judah	Condemnation of wicked; worship; restoration; everlasting deliverance, everlasting judgment.
Jeremiah	Pre-exile 6th/7th cent. BC	Judah	Warnings and exhortations; his suffering; fall of Jerusalem; judgment against nations.
Lamentations (Jeremiah)	Pre-exile/exile c. 580 BC	Judah	Laments over destruction of Jerusalem.
Ezekiel	Exile 6th cent. BC	Jews in Babylon	God's sovereignty over creation, people, nations, and history; God's holiness; judgment against Judah and pagan nations; God's future work in history.
Daniel	Exile c. 530 BC	Jews in Babylon	Prayer, spiritual warfare, living by God's standards in a hostile environment, God's sovereignty.
Hosea	Pre-exile 8th cent. BC	Israel	Just as Hosea is betrayed by his beloved, God is betrayed by his beloved Israel. Loving commitment can overcome betrayal.
Joel	Pre-exile Uncertain	Judah	God's people have a choice: keep doing wrong and be judged, or repent and receive God's forgiveness and salvation.

Book	Era	Audience	Theme(s)
Amos	Pre-exile 8th cent. BC	Israel	Israel ignores what matters to God – justice, compassion, and worship from the heart – and God's impending judgment.
Obadiah	Pre-exile c. 587 BC	Edom	Edomites, who treated Israel unjustly, now face God's anger.
Jonah	Pre-exile 8th cent. BC	Assyria	God's forgiveness of us, our need to forgive others.
Micah	Pre-exile 8th cent. BC	Judah	God's judgment for idolatry and oppression; his mercy for the obedient; our need to show mercy; the coming Messiah.
Nahum	Pre-exile 7th cent. BC	Assyria	The judgment of Assyria and its capital, Nineveh.
Habakkuk	Pre-exile 7th cent. BC	Judah	Is God ignoring evil, or will he settle the score?
Zephaniah	Pre-exile 7th cent. BC	Judah	Judgment day is coming; closing promise.
Haggai	Post-exile 6th cent. BC	Jews in Jerusalem	God's blessings, and what the Jews did to hinder them; rebuild the temple.
Zechariah	Post-exile 6th/5th cent. BC ?	Jews in Jerusalem	God's encouragement to exiles who returned from Babylon; prophecies about the coming Messiah; salvation.
Malachi	Post-exile 5th/4th cent. BC ?	Jews in Jerusalem	God's readiness to replace the old covenant with the new; prophecies about the Messiah, who will usher in the new covenant.

[Source information: **Zondervan Handbook of the Bible**, 411, and the author.]

Read This Week

Pages 756–839 in *NIV Bible in 90 Days* (Dan. 9:1–Matt. 26:56)

You are about to read a marathon of prophets; the preceding chart will help you recognize key themes in these books.

Personal Progress

If it is helpful to do so, use the following chart to record your reading progress this week. Establish a reading schedule that works well for you—then stick with it.

✓	Day	Pages in the *NIV Bible in 90 Days*	Passage begins:
	1 (Today)	756 – 768	Daniel 9:1
	2	768 – 780	Hosea 13:7
	3	781 – 792	Amos 9:11
	4	792 – 805	Habakkuk 1:1
	5	805 – 815	Zechariah 11:1
	6	816 – 828	Matthew 5:1
	7	828 – 840	Matthew 16:1

If you are behind in your reading, set aside extra time this week to catch up.

Personal Reading Notes

Take a moment to record the highlights — knowledge gained, puzzling questions, "aha! moments" — you experience during your reading this week.

Try It!

Memorize the names of the first five books of the New Testament:

M_____   M_____

L_____   J_____

A_____

READING OUTLINE

Discuss Today: pages 756–840 of *NIV Bible in 90 Days* (Dan. 9:1–Matt. 26:56)

Reading for the Coming Week: pages 840–924 of *NIV Bible in 90 Days* (Matt. 26:57–Acts 6:7)

SMALL GROUP DISCUSSION

Reading Follow-up

1. How was your reading this week? What new challenges did you face in accomplishing your reading? What was the most effective thing you did to meet those challenges?

2. As you read the Bible this week, which particular thought(s) and/ or event(s) stood out to you or surprised you? Why?

3. Which question(s) came up during your reading for which you'd like to find answers?

4. In what ways is your reading affecting your view of God, his Word, and your relationship with him?

Reading Discovery

Note: The following explanation and questions are intended to stimulate discussion. There is no need to answer the questions prior to your class or small group meeting.

Welcome to the New Testament!

The Old Testament story covers a time span of about two thousand years. At the end of that time, God severely punished and scattered his people because they had repeatedly failed to obey the covenant he had made with them. For the next four hundred years — what some historians call the "silent years" — we have no new, God-inspired writings.

The Jewish faith continued to evolve during this time, however. The Jews returned to the land of Israel and worshiped in local synagogues. They continued to sacrifice and worship in the temple King Herod built in Jerusalem. They followed laws of circumcision, Sabbath keeping, and Levitical food requirements. Jewish scholars also produced the Septuagint — a Greek translation of the first five books of the Bible (Torah).

By the first century AD, the Jews had divided into several sects, each with its own beliefs and traditions regarding the law. One dominant sect, the Pharisees, strictly adhered to legalistic traditions. They tried to reinterpret the law of Moses so that, given all the changes since Moses' day, they could live righteously before God (*NIV Study Bible*, note for Acts 15:1). They believed in angels, demons, resurrection of the dead, and immortality. Aristocratic Sadducees, the dominant ruling sect at the time, controlled the temple's organization (including the high priesthood) and the Sanhedrin (the Jewish Supreme Council). The Sadducees were exacting in Levitical purity and interpreted the Mosaic law more literally than the Pharisees. They rejected belief in angels, demons, resurrection of the dead, and immortality.

Into this confusion and power struggle within the Jewish faith, God once again made his presence known in human history. God fulfilled the Old Testament promises by sending the long-awaited Son of David, Jesus Christ the Messiah. As Matthew so carefully explains, Jesus came not only to communicate God's truth but to establish a new covenant with all who would be God's people. It's not surprising, then, that the book of Matthew — the first book of the New Testament and the first of four gospels that tell us about Jesus' life, ministry, and purpose — begins with the Davidic lineage of Jesus to show to Jewish readers that Jesus fulfilled the Old Testament's predictions and that God was ushering in a new covenant.

Matthew provides the details on how God sent his Son, the Messiah, to provide the way for all people — Jew and Gentile alike — to receive eternal life through the life, death, and resurrection of Jesus. Matthew presents the complete plan of salvation according to the new covenant, a covenant that is written on the heart and produces a new spiritual life based not on the external evidence of obedience but on the life of the Spirit within. And Matthew proclaims the promise that one day Jesus the Messiah will return to earth and make all things new.

1. As you read the "minor" prophets, which themes kept coming up? What did you learn about the character of God and Israel's wrongdoing and future hope?

2. In what way(s) have you benefited from your Old Testament reading?

3. In what ways has your Old Testament reading helped you understand why Matthew began his book with the genealogy of Jesus? Why is it significant that Matthew emphasized Jesus' identity as the Messiah and the King of the Jews?

4. As he taught his disciples, Jesus repeatedly referred to or quoted Old Testament passages of Scripture. Why do you think he did this?

5. When Jesus taught, he often emphasized the importance of a heart commitment rather than mere obedience to man-made rules and traditions. Why was this such an important truth for his Jewish audience to understand?

Did You Know?

- Herod's temple, where the Jews of Jesus' day worshiped, towered high above the surrounding countryside and was built on the same site as the temples built by Solomon and Zerubbabel. Its Holy Place and Most Holy Place had the same floor dimensions as the temple Solomon built. Construction of the fifteen-story temple began in 20 BC, and the Romans tore it down in AD 70 (*NIV Study Bible*, 1473) after the great Jewish revolt erupted in AD 66 (*Handbook*, 535).

- The star of Bethlehem that pinpointed Jesus' location had newly appeared, traveled slowly, and "stood over" Bethlehem. According to scholars, only a comet with a long tail could satisfy these criteria. The Chinese, who closely watched stars and comets, observed a spectacular comet that appeared in 5 BC and remained visible for more than seventy days. Data from the Chinese records indicates that the Magi would first have seen this comet in the east, just as Matthew described (*Handbook*, 553).

- Matthew included nine proof texts that occur only in his gospel to show that Jesus Christ fulfilled the Old Testament Scriptures: see verses 1:22 – 23; 2:15; 2:17 – 18; 2:23; 4:14 – 16; 8:17; 12:17 – 21; 13:35; 27:9 – 10 (*NIV Study Bible*, 1463). Matthew also focused on Jesus' role as "Son of David" in such verses as 1:1; 9:27; 12:23; 15:22; and 20:30 – 31. These help show that Jesus fulfilled the covenant God made with Abraham (Gen. 12:2 – 3; 15:9 – 21) (*NIV Study Bible*, note for Matt. 1:1).

VIDEO NOTES

1. As you watched the video, which particular point(s) stood out to you? Why?

2. Which aspect of the video particularly enhanced your understanding of what you read this past week?

3. What would you identify as the key themes of this portion of Scripture?

4. What impact can what you've just seen make on your life today?

ON YOUR OWN BETWEEN SESSIONS

This Week's Reading Tip

You will experience some repetition in your reading this week.
Pay attention to the similarities and differences
in the various authors' accounts.

The Gospels Overview

Matthew, the tax collector called to be a disciple, was a Jew who wrote his gospel to other Jews around AD 60 in order to proclaim Jesus as the promised Messiah, the King of the Jews. He shows how Jesus came to fulfill the Old Testament, but also to judge the Jews for their unfaithfulness (it's the gospel that most strongly condemns the hypocritical Pharisees). Although many stories and events recorded in Matthew are found only here in the gospels, most noted is Jesus' Sermon on the Mount (chs. 5–7).

Mark, the same John Mark of Acts and the New Testament letters who accompanied the apostle Paul on missionary journeys, was a Roman who wrote his gospel to other Romans around AD 55 to proclaim Jesus as a man of action. His account moves rapidly from one episode in Jesus' life and ministry to another, emphasizing more what he did than what he said. He emphasizes how Jesus taught his disciples that the "son of man" must suffer and be rejected, and that they must be prepared to walk the same path.

Luke, a physician who also authored the book of Acts, was a Greek who wrote his gospel to other Greeks around AD 58 in order to proclaim Jesus as the perfect man. Presenting the works and teachings of Jesus most essential for understanding the way of salvation, Luke focuses on the grace of God revealed in Jesus and given to those—for example, prostitutes and tax collectors—who seem least worthy to receive it.

John, called "the disciple whom Jesus loved" (see John 13:23 and elsewhere), wrote his gospel to all people around AD 85 in order to proclaim Jesus as the Son of God, operating with his Father's full authority. The most unique of the gospel accounts, John's gospel goes deepest theologically, touching on issues such as the incarnation (ch. 1)

and the ministry of the Holy Spirit (chs. 14–16). Also look for Jesus'
seven "I am" statements here: the bread of life; the light of the world;
the gate for the sheep; the good shepherd; the resurrection and the life;
the way, truth, and life; and the true vine.

Acts Overview

Written by Luke, the book of Acts begins with the post-resurrection
appearance of Jesus to his disciples, then fast-forwards to his dramatic
ascension to heaven and the day of Pentecost. From that point on, the
fledgling church takes up its call to be Jesus' "witnesses in Jerusalem,
and in all Judea and Samaria, and to the ends of the earth" (Acts 1:8).

Read This Week

Pages 840–924 of the *NIV Bible in 90 Days* (Matt. 26:57–Acts 6:7)

Personal Progress

If it is helpful to do so, use the following chart to record your reading progress this week. Establish a reading schedule that works well
for you—then stick with it.

✓	Day	Pages in the *NIV Bible in 90 Days*	Passage begins:
	1 (Today)	840–852	Matthew 26:57
	2	852–864	Mark 9:14
	3	864–876	Luke 2:1
	4	876–888	Luke 10:1
	5	888–900	Luke 20:20
	6	900–912	John 6:1
	7	912–924	John 15:18

If you are behind in your reading, set aside extra time this week to
catch up.

Personal Reading Notes

Take a moment to record the highlights—knowledge gained, puzzling questions, "aha! moments"—you experience during your reading this week.

Try It!

Memorize the names of the next six books of the New Testament:

R_____   1 C_____

2 C_____   G_____

E_____   P_____

After you've mastered the names above, try recalling all the New Testament books you've memorized thus far.

READING OUTLINE

Discuss Today: pages 840 – 924 of *NIV Bible in 90 Days* (Matt. 26:57 – Acts 6:7)

Reading for the Coming Week: pages 924 – 1008 of *NIV Bible in 90 Days* (Acts 6:8 – Philem. 25)

SMALL GROUP DISCUSSION

Reading Follow-up

1. How was your reading this week? What new challenges did you face in accomplishing your reading? What was the most effective thing you did to meet those challenges?

2. As you read the Bible this week, which particular thought(s) and/ or event(s) stood out to you or surprised you? What question(s) do you have regarding your reading?

3. In what ways has your reading of the Old Testament enhanced your understanding of the events and people you are reading about in the New Testament?

4. In what ways is your reading affecting your view of God, his Word, and your relationship with him?

Reading Discovery

Note: The following questions are intended to stimulate discussion. There is no need to answer them prior to your class or small group meeting.

1. Why is the death and resurrection of Jesus so important? What did these events accomplish for the Jews of Jesus' day and for you?

2. What do the Gospels reveal about the humanity and deity of Jesus?

3. What are some of the things you noticed Jesus said about himself? Why are these statements significant?

4. Identify several truths that Jesus repeatedly tried to teach his disciples but that they just didn't seem to "get." In contrast, in what ways did Jesus' disciples demonstrate spiritual growth the longer they knew him?

5. What do the Gospels reveal about the suffering of Jesus and his disciples, and the costs of discipleship?

6. Now that you have read all four Gospels, discuss the following portraits of Jesus:

• Matthew: Jesus as the King of the Jews

• Mark: Jesus as a servant

• Luke: Jesus as the perfect man

• John: Jesus as the Son of God

Did You Know?

- When John the Baptist called Jesus "the Lamb of God," he used a phrase that related to the Old Testament sacrifices. (See Lev. 4:32 – 35; Isa. 53:4 – 12.) Whereas in Old Testament times an animal could be sacrificed as an atonement for the sin that separated a person from the holy God, Jesus came to earth as God's "Lamb" and shed his blood to remove the sins of the entire world. (See Lev. 17:11; *Handbook*, 623.)

- When Jesus walked its streets, the city of Jerusalem was much larger than it had been during the days of King David. The wealthier people lived in a newer Upper City section west of the former City of David. The temple bordered the northern boundary of David's former city and overlooked the Mount of Olives and Garden of Gethsemane to the east. It accounted for about a fifth of the city. Herod's palace was in the upper western corner of the Upper City. Golgotha, the traditional site of Jesus' crucifixion, was just north of Herod's place outside the city wall (*Handbook*, 630).

- When Jesus taught, he often used images familiar to his audience. For example, while in Jerusalem during the Feast of Shelters, he identified himself as "the light of the world." This was meaningful because at dusk feast participants held a ceremony in which four golden candelabra were lit. These symbolized the pillar of fire God used to guide his people through the desert wilderness at night.

- One way to gain a picture of the whole of Scripture is to think of it this way: the Old Testament — a record of God the Father; the Gospels — a record of God the Son; and Acts through Revelation — a record of God the Spirit.

VIDEO DISCUSSION (OPTIONAL)

1. As you watched the video, which particular point(s) stood out to you? Why?

2. Which aspect of the video particularly enhanced your understanding of what you read this past week?

3. What would you identify as the key themes of this portion of Scripture?

4. What impact can what you've just seen make on your life today?

ON YOUR OWN BETWEEN SESSIONS

This Week's Reading Tip

This week you'll read all of Paul's letters to various churches and disciples, which is among the most personal and distinctive writing in all of Scripture. Enjoy it!

Acts Overview

In this sequel to the gospel of Luke, notice the powerful work of the Holy Spirit in the lives of Christ's followers as they fulfill Christ's command to be his witnesses to the ends of the earth.

Romans through Philemon Overview

Notice the predominant theme(s) in each of Paul's letters. Pay attention to how often he emphasized the fundamentals of Christian belief, especially that faith in Christ's death and resurrection is the only ground for salvation by God. Also take note of his personal and distinctive style of writing and the practical guidance and advice he offered his readers — including us today.

Read This Week

Pages 924–1008 of *NIV Bible in 90 Days* (Acts 6:8–Philem. 25)

Personal Progress

If it is helpful to do so, use the following chart to record your reading progress this week. Establish a reading schedule that works well for you — then stick with it.

✓	Day	Pages in the *NIV Bible in 90 Days*	Passage begins:
	1 (Today)	924–936	Acts 6:8
	2	936–948	Acts 16:38
	3	948–960	Acts 28:17
	4	960–972	Romans 15:1
	5	972–984	1 Corinthians 15:1
	6	984–996	Galatians 3:26
	7	997–1008	1 Thessalonians 1:1

If you are behind in your reading, set aside extra time this week to catch up.

Personal Reading Notes

Take a moment to record the highlights—knowledge gained, puzzling questions, "aha! moments"—you experience during your reading this week.

Try It!

Memorize the names of the next seven books of the New Testament:

C_____   1 T_____

2 T_____   1 T_____

2 T_____   T_____

P_____

After you've mastered the names above, try recalling all the New Testament books you've memorized thus far.

READING OUTLINE

Discuss Today: pages 924 – 1008 of *NIV Bible in 90 Days* (Acts 6:8 – Philem. 25)

Reading for This Week: pages 1009 – 1048 in *NIV Bible in 90 Days* (Heb. 1:1 – Rev. 22:21)

SMALL GROUP DISCUSSION

Reading Follow-up

1. How was your reading this week? What new challenges did you face in accomplishing your reading? What was the most effective thing you did to meet those challenges?

2. As you read the Bible this week, which particular thought(s) and/ or event(s) stood out to you or surprised you? What question(s) do you have regarding your reading?

3. In what ways has your reading of the Old Testament enhanced your understanding of the events and people you are reading about in the New Testament?

4. In what ways is your reading affecting your view of God, his Word, and your relationship with him?

Reading Discovery

Note: The following questions are intended to stimulate discussion. There is no need to answer them prior to your class or small group meeting.

1. Which accounts of the experiences of the early Christians, and which individual Christians, do you find most remarkable? Why?

2. What did you learn in Paul's letters about the early churches? Why was Paul concerned about them? As you read Paul's instructions to these churches, what did you learn about integrating faith with everyday life?

3. Second Timothy 3:16–17 is at the heart of why it is important to read the Bible. In what ways has reading the Bible proved to be useful and made you better equipped for every good work?

4. What are some of the ways by which the apostles made Christ known to people in various walks of life? In what ways can you apply their example to life in your world?

5. Why do you think Paul emphasized faith in Christ's death and resurrection as the only grounds of acceptance by God? Why was it important for believers to stop clinging to religious traditions and to rely on what Jesus accomplished through his death and resurrection?

6. In what ways have this week's readings influenced your thoughts on a current event or personal experience? Which of Paul's instructions particularly apply to the above event or experience?

Did You Know?

- The early Christians, believing that the long-awaited coming of Jesus fulfilled ancient Old Testament prophecies regarding the Messiah, viewed themselves as participants in the ongoing story of God's dealings with humankind. Jesus — God in human form — had come to earth personally to rescue all of humanity from sinful rebellion. No wonder these Christians studied the Old Testament diligently! No wonder they joyously proclaimed him and his message to people everywhere so that the news spread throughout the world. No wonder they rejoiced in the eternal life they would one day receive.

- In Acts 17:5 – 8, we read that angry Jews in ancient Thessalonica dragged some Christians before the city officials. It is interesting to note that in this instance the Greek word translated "city ruler," *politarch*, has not been found anywhere else in Greek literature. But in 1835, this word was discovered on an ancient arch that spanned the Egnatian Way on the west side of Thessalonica. In 1867, the arch was destroyed, but the block containing the inscription is in the British Museum in London (*NIV Study Bible*, note for Acts 17:6).

- New Christians in the Greek city of Corinth faced great temptations and challenges as they learned to follow Christ. At least twelve pagan temples were located there, including one dedicated to Aphrodite, the goddess of love and sex. Followers of Aphrodite worshiped her by practicing religious prostitution with as many as one thousand sacred priestesses. Immorality in Corinth became so rampant that the Greek verb translated "to Corinthianize" came to mean "to practice sexual immorality" (*NIV Study Bible*, 1774, and notes for 1 Cor. 6:18; 7:2).

WHOLE GROUP DISCUSSION: FINISHING STRONG

ON YOUR OWN BETWEEN SESSIONS

This Week's Reading Tip

Good news ... you have only forty pages to read this week! So if you are a few pages behind, you have a great opportunity to catch up and complete your commitment to reading the entire Bible.

Hebrews Overview

As you read Hebrews, which some view as a condensation of the entire Bible, pay close attention to the themes relating to Jesus' identity and accomplishments. Note his position as our "great high priest," the new covenant he established, and the call to follow him faithfully. Carefully observe the many Old Testament references the writer uses.

James Overview

One of the earliest books of the New Testament, James includes practical teaching about putting faith into action. It includes instruction on temptations, faith, taming the tongue, worldliness, and oppression.

1 – 2 Peter Overview

As you read, look for what God may want to reveal to you about living wholeheartedly for him, particularly in the areas of personal holiness, submission to authority, and humility. Consider, too, Peter's warnings about false teachers and being prepared for the second coming of Christ.

1, 2, 3 John Overview

Keep in mind that John, an apostle in Jesus' inner circle, was writing to believers who were confronting heretical Gnostic teaching. Notice the powerful themes of God's love and faith that lead to obedience.

Jude Overview

In this short book of encouragement to persevere in faith, warnings against false teachers are prominent.

Revelation Overview

Written to encourage God's faithful people during a time of increasing persecution, this book presents a look at the triumph that is to come. Notice, among such end-time themes as Christ's return and Satan's doom, the increasing urgency of God's call to repentance.

Read This Week

Pages 1009 – 1048 of *NIV Bible in 90 Days* (Heb. 1:1 – Rev. 22:21)

Personal Progress

If it is helpful to do so, use the following chart to record your reading progress this week.

✓	Day	Pages in the *NIV Bible in 90 Days*	Passage begins:
	1 (Today)	1009 - 1020	Hebrews 1:1
	2	1020 - 1032	James 3:13
	3	1032 - 1044	Jude 1
	4	1044 - 1048	Revelation 18:1

If you are behind in your reading, set aside extra time this week to catch up.

Personal Reading Notes

Take a moment to record the highlights—knowledge gained, puzzling questions, "aha! moments"—you experienced during your reading this week.

Try It!

Memorize the names of the last nine books of the New Testament:

H_____   J_____

1 P_____   2 P_____

1 J_____   2 J_____

3 J_____   J_____

R_____

After you've mastered the names above, try recalling all the New Testament books you've memorized thus far.

VIDEO NOTES

Did You Know?

- During New Testament times, it is likely that more Jews lived in other countries than in their homeland. (An estimated one million lived in Egypt, for example.) Political tensions between the Romans and Jews continued and intensified after Jesus' death and resurrection. The Jews made their last stand against the Romans during the Jewish War, AD 66–73, during which time the Romans destroyed the temple. The remaining Jews scattered to other countries where, in colonies in various cities, they maintained their distinctive culture and lifestyle. In his travels, the apostle Paul made a point of visiting these expatriate Jewish communities to share the transforming message of Jesus (*Handbook*, 753).

- The seven churches mentioned in Revelation 2 and 3 were located in places we can identify:

  1. *Ephesus*, an ancient city in the Roman province of Asia, was Paul's home for two years during his third missionary tour. The church here lacked love.

  2. *Smyrna*, a small church in what is now named Izmir in western Turkey, lacked money but was spiritually rich.

  3. *Pergamum*, near the modern-day town of Bergama in western Turkey, was a center of emperor worship and had a huge altar dedicated to Zeus. As false teaching crept into this church, so did pagan practices.

  4. *Thyatira*, now the small town of Akhisar in western Turkey, had many skilled workers and was known for its purple dye. Many people within the church fell into immorality through the influence of a woman in the fellowship.

  5. *Sardis*, the capital of ancient Lydia, is about fifty miles east of Smyrna. Once home to rich King Croesus, it had both a Jewish synagogue and a large Greek temple. The church here suffered from self-satisfaction and apathy.

  6. *Philadelphia*, about twenty-eight miles southeast of Sardis in present-day Turkey, was located near a broad and fertile valley. The church here was faithful.

  7. *Laodicea*, now named Latakia in Syria, was a prosperous banking center known for its eye salve and fine wool. The city, which had no water supply of its own, used lukewarm water channeled from hot springs in nearby Hierapolis. The church here was lukewarm—blind to its true spiritual condition (*Handbook*, 767–769).

RESPONSIVE READING FROM REVELATION 21 – 22

Then I saw a new heaven and a new earth, for the first heaven and the first earth had passed away, and there was no longer any sea. I saw the Holy City, the new Jerusalem, coming down out of heaven from God, prepared as a bride beautifully dressed for her husband. And I heard a loud voice from the throne saying, "Now the dwelling of God is with men, and he will live with them. They will be his people, and God himself will be with them and be their God. He will wipe every tear from their eyes. There will be no more death or mourning or crying or pain, for the old order of things has passed away" (21:1–4).

Thank you, Lord, for your desire to live with us. Thank you for your faithfulness to us despite our unfaithfulness. Thank you for all you have done over thousands of years to make life with you possible.

He who was seated on the throne said, "I am making everything new!" Then he said, "Write this down, for these words are trustworthy and true."

He said to me: "It is done. I am the Alpha and the Omega, the Beginning and the End. To him who is thirsty I will give to drink without cost from the spring of the water of life. He who overcomes will inherit all this, and I will be his God and he will be my son. But the cowardly, the unbelieving, the vile, the murderers, the sexually immoral, those who practice magic arts, the idolaters and all liars—their place will be in the fiery lake of burning sulfur. This is the second death" (21:5–8).

Praise you, Lord, for your eternal presence. Praise you for making all things new. Thank you for sharing with us the cup of eternal life.

I, John, am the one who heard and saw these things. And when I had heard and seen them, I fell down to worship at the feet of the angel who had been showing them to me. But he said to me, "Do not do it! I am a fellow servant with you and with your brothers the prophets and of all who keep the words of this book. Worship God!"

Then he told me, "Do not seal up the words of the prophecy of this book, because the time is near" (22:8–10).

Praise you, Lord, for your words of truth. We worship you.

"Behold, I am coming soon! My reward is with me, and I will give to everyone according to what he has done. I am the Alpha and the Omega, the First and the Last, the Beginning and the End.

"Blessed are those who wash their robes, that they may have the right to the tree of life and may go through the gates into the city. Outside are the dogs, those who practice magic arts, the sexually immoral, the murderers, the idolaters and everyone who loves and practices falsehood.

"I, Jesus, have sent my angel to give you this testimony for the churches. I am the Root and the Offspring of David, and the bright Morning Star."

The Spirit and the bride say, "Come!" And let him who hears say, "Come!" Whoever is thirsty, let him come; and whoever wishes, let him take the free gift of the water of life (22:12–17).

Praise you, Lord, for sending Jesus, son of David, holy Lamb of God, to cleanse us from our sin.

I warn everyone who hears the words of the prophecy of this book: If anyone adds anything to them, God will add to him the plagues described in this book. And if anyone takes words away from this book of prophecy, God will take away from him his share in the tree of life and in the holy city, which are described in this book.

He who testifies to these things says, "Yes, I am coming soon."
Amen. Come, Lord Jesus.
The grace of the Lord Jesus be with God's people. Amen (22:18–21).

Bless your name, Lord Jesus! We wait for you.

THE BIBLE IN 90 DAYS™ LISTENING PLAN

If you would rather listen to the Bible than read, that option is also available using one of two audio products:

Using the *NIV Dramatized Audio Bible on 64 Audio CDs*, listeners will "read" the entire Bible in 88 days with 2 "grace" days allowed during the period.

Day	Start Verse	Start	End Verse	End	Run Time
1	Ge 1:1	OT-1, Track 1 0:00	Ge 16:16	OT-1, Track 19 2:09 (end)	58:22
2	Ge 17:1	OT-1, Track 20 0:00	Ge 28:19	OT-2, Track 9 2:49	53:33
3	Ge 28:20	OT-2, Track 9 2:49	Ge 40:11	OT-3, Track 6 1:16	50:56
4	Ge 40:12	OT-3, Track 6 1:16	Ge 50:26	OT-3, Track 16 3:50 (end)	49:08
5	Ex 1:1	OT-4, Track 1 0:00	Ex 15:18	OT-4, Track 16 3:11	61:27
6	Ex 15:19	OT-4, Track 16 3:11	Ex 28:43	OT-5, Track 12 5:55 (end)	53:52
7	Ex 29:1	OT-5, Track 13 0:00	Ex 40:38	OT-6, Track 7 3:58 (end)	53:10
8	Le 1:1	OT-6, Track 8 0:00	Le 14:32	OT-7, Track 5 4:54	61:45
9	Le 14:33	OT-7, Track 5 4:54	Le 26:26	OT-8, Track 3 3:40	57:51
10	Le 26:27	OT-8, Track 3 3:40	Nu 8:14	OT-8, Track 13 1:39	52:59
11	Nu 8:15	OT-8, Track 13 1:39	Nu 21:7	OT-9, Track 13 1:06	54:39
12	Nu 21:8	OT-9, Track 13 1:06	Nu 32:19	OT-10, Track 8 2:33	49:57
13	Nu 32:20	OT-10, Track 8 2:33	Dt 7:26	OT-11, Track 4 4:50(end)	59:32
14	Dt 8:1	OT-11, Track 5 0:00	Dt 23:11	OT-12, Track 4 1:30	62:38
15	Dt 23:12	OT-12, Track 4 1:30	Dt 34:12	OT-12, Track 15 1:54 (end)	61:28
16	Jos 1:1	OT-13, Track 1 0:00	Jos 14:15	OT-13, Track 15 2:32 (end)	56:09
17	Jos 15:1	OT-13, Track 16 0:00	Jdg 3:27	OT-14, Track 10 3:38	56:26
18	Jdg 3:28	OT-14, Track 10 3:38	Jdg 15:12	OT-15, Track 6 1:52	51:10
19	Jdg 15:13	OT-15, Track 6 1:52	1Sa 2:29	OT-16, Track 1 4:36	51:49
20	1Sa 2:30	OT-16, Track 1 4:36	1Sa 15:35	OT-16, Track 14 5:14 (end)	51:17
21	1Sa 16:1	OT-16, Track 15 0:00	1Sa 28:19	OT-17, Track 11 2:53	53:42
22	1Sa 28:20	OT-17, Track 11 2:53	2Sa 12:10	OT-18, Track 9 1:43	52:26

Day	Start Verse	Start	End Verse	End	Run Time
23	2Sa 12:11	OT-18, Track 9 1:43	2Sa 22:18	OT-19, Track 3 1:58	53:17
24	2Sa 22:19	OT-19, Track 3 1:58	1Ki 7:37	OT-19, Track 13 5:08	52:04
25	1Ki 7:38	OT-19, Track 13 5:08	1Ki 16:20	OT-20, Track 9 3:07	51:50
26	1Ki 16:21	OT-20, Track 9 3:07	2Ki 4:37	OT-21, Track 7 5:05	53:18
27	2Ki 4:38	OT-21, Track 7 5:05	2Ki 15:26	OT-22, Track 3 4:11	53:49
28	2Ki 15:27	OT-22, Track 3 4:11	2Ki 25:30	OT-22, Track 13 4:50 (end)	51:29
29	1Ch 1:1	OT-23, Track 1 0:00	1Ch 9:44	OT-23, Track 10 6:05 (end)	52:06
30	1Ch 10:1	OT-23, Track 11 0:00	1Ch 23:32	OT-24, Track 9 4:28 (end)	52:21
31	1Ch 24:1	OT-24, Track 10 0:00	2Ch 7:10	OT-25, Track 4 1:47	52:40
32	2Ch 7:11	OT-25, Track 4 1:47	2Ch 23:15	OT-26, Track 1 2:54	53:32
33	2Ch 23:16	OT-26, Track 1 2:54	2Ch 35:15	OT-26, Track 13 2:49	54:27
34	2Ch 35:16	OT-26, Track 13 2:49	Ez 10:44	OT-27, Track 8 6:18 (end)	48:34
35	Ne 1:1	OT-27, Track 9 0:00	Ne 13:14	OT-28, Track 4 2:27	60:04
36	Ne 13:15	OT-28, Track 4 2:27	Job 7:21	OT-28, Track 23 2:24 (end)	52:32
37	Job 8:1	OT-28, Track 24 0:00	Job 24:25	OT-29, Track 16 3:01 (end)	41:49
38	Job 25:1	OT-29, Track 17 0:00	Job 41:34	OT-30, Track 4 2:57 (end)	42:55
39	Job 42:1	OT-30, Track 5 0:00	Ps 24:10	OT-30, Track 30 1:08 (end)	39:37
40	Ps 25:1	OT-30, Track 31 0:00	Ps 45:14	OT-31, Track 10 2:07	41:20
41	Ps 45:15	OT-31, Track 10 2:07	Ps 69:21	OT-31, Track 34 2:36	42:11
42	Ps 69:22	OT-31, Track 34 2:36	Ps 89:13	OT-32, Track 16 1:35	45:20
43	Ps 89:14	OT-32, Track 16 1:35	Ps 108:13	OT-33, Track 2 1:18 (end)	43:31
44	Ps 109:1	OT-33, Track 3 0:00	Ps 134:3	OT-33, Track 28 0:18 (end)	41:00
45	Ps 135:1	OT-33, Track 29 0:00	Pr 6:35	OT-34, Track 7 3:17 (end)	41:00
46	Pr 7:1	OT-34, Track 8 0:00	Pr 20:21	OT-34, Track 21 2:07	39:00
47	Pr 20:22	OT-34, Track 21 2:07	Ecc 2:26	OT-35, Track 9 3:50 (end)	42:11
48	Ecc 3:1	OT-35, Track 10 0:00	SoS 8:14	OT-35, Track 28 2:01 (end)	41:07
49	Isa 1:1	OT-35, Track 29 0:00	Isa 13:22	OT-36, Track 12 3:10 (end)	43:59
50	Isa 14:1	OT-36, Track 13 0:00	Isa 28:29	OT-37, Track 3 5:16 (end)	44:40
51	Isa 29:1	OT-37, Track 4 0:00	Isa 41:18	OT-37, Track 16 3:06	45:33
52	Isa 41:19	OT-37, Track 16 3:06	Isa 52:12	OT-38, Track 8 2:17	45:33
53	Isa 52:13	OT-38, Track 8 2:17	Isa 66:18	OT-38, Track 22 3:55	44:07
54	Isa 66:19	OT-38, Track 22 3:55	Jer 10:13	OT-39, Track 11 1:55	46:56
55	Jer 10:14	OT-39, Track 11 1:55	Jer 23:8	OT-40, Track 6 1:30	45:51
56	Jer 23:9	OT-40, Track 6 1:30	Jer 33:22	OT-40, Track 16 3:42	49:48
57	Jer 33:23	OT-40, Track 16 3:42	Jer 47:7	OT-41, Track 14 1:08 (end)	46:32
58	Jer 48:1	OT-41, Track 15 0:00	La 1:22	OT-42, Track 4 4:59 (end)	40:50

Day	Start Verse	Start	End Verse	End	Run Time
59	La 2:1	OT-42, Track 5 0:00	Eze 12:20	OT-43, Track 1 3:23	61:52
60	Eze 12:21	OT-43, Track 1 3:23	Eze 23:39	OT-43, Track 12 6:19	60:28
61	Eze 23:40	OT-43, Track 12 6:19	Eze 35:15	OT-44, Track 11 2:41 (end)	56:38
62	Eze 36:1	OT-44, Track 12 0:00	Eze 47:12	OT-45, Track 8 2:01	59:17
63	Eze 47:13	OT-45, Track 8 2:01	Da 8:27	OT-46, Track 3 4:19 (end)	48:57
64	Da 9:1	OT-46, Track 4 0:00	Hos 13:6	OT-46, Track 21 0:55	45:21
65	Hos 13:7	OT-46, Track 21 0:55	Am 9:10	OT-47, Track 11 2:11	40:20
66	Am 9:11	OT-47, Track 11 2:11	Nah 3:19	OT-47, Track 30 3:10 (end)	44:32
67	Hab 1:1	OT-48, Track 1 0:00	Zec 10:12	OT-48, Track 22 2:08 (end)	51:25
68	Zec 11:1	OT-48, Track 23 0:00	Mt 4:25	NT-1, Track 6 3:33 (end)	38:12
69	Mt 5:1	NT-1, Track 7 0:00	Mt 15:39	NT-2, Track 1 2:26 (end)	59:28
70	Mt 16:1	NT-2, Track 2 0:00	Mt 26:56	NT-2, Track 12 7:42	59:07
71	Mt 26:57	NT-2, Track 12 7:42	Mk 9:13	NT-3, Track 11 1:42	57:19
72	Mk 9:14	NT-3, Track 11 1:42	Lk 1:00	NT-4, Track 5 9:31 (end)	57:10
73	Lk 2:1	NT-4, Track 6 0:00	Lk 9:62	NT-5, Track 2 8:50 (end)	57:12
74	Lk 10:1	NT-5, Track 3 0:00	Lk 20:19	NT-6, Track 2 2:33	59:43
75	Lk 20:20	NT-6, Track 2 2:33	Jn 5:47	NT-6, Track 12 5:49 (end)	57:40
76	Jn 6:1	NT-6, Track 13 0:00	Jn 15:17	NT-7, Track 9 2:27	56:46
77	Jn 15:18	NT-7, Track 9 2:27	Ac 6:7	NT-8, Track 8 1:02	50:54
78	Ac 6:8	NT-8, Track 8 1:02	Ac 16:37	NT-9, Track 1 5:01	50:42
79	Ac 16:38	NT-9, Track 1 5:01	Ac 28:16	NT-9, Track 13 2:07	55:07
80	Ac 28:17	NT-9, Track 13 2:07	Ro 14:23	NT-10, Track 13 3:27 (end)	59:54
81	Ro 15:1	NT-10, Track 14 0:00	1Co 14:40	NT-11, Track 10 5:19 (end)	59:01
82	1Co 15:1	NT-11, Track 11 0:00	Gal 3:25	NT-12, Track 8 3:49	61:13
83	Gal 3:26	NT-12, Track 8 3:49	Col 4:18	NT-13, Track 7 2:25 (end)	61:31
84	1Th 1:1	NT-13, Track 8 0:00	Phm 25	NT-14, Track 8 3:01 (end)	61:57
85	Heb 1:1	NT-14, Track 9 0:00	Jas 3:12	NT-15, Track 2 1:46	56:36
86	Jas 3:13	NT-15, Track 2 1:46	3Jn 14	NT-15, Track 24 2:06 (end)	59:25
87	Jude 1	NT-15, Track 25 0:00	Rev 17:18	NT-16, Track 17 3:35 (end)	62:03
88	Rev 18:1	NT-16, Track 18 0:00	Rev 22:21	NT-16, Track 22 4:02 (end)	20:13
89					
90					

Using the *NIV Dramatized Audio Bible on 6 MP3 CDs*, listeners will "read" through the entire Bible in 88 days with 2 "grace" days allowed during the period.

Day	Start Verse	Start	End Verse	End	Run Time
1	Ge 1:1	Disc 1, Track 1 0:00	Ge 16:16	Disc 1, Track 19 2:09 (end)	58:22
2	Ge 17:1	Disc 1, Track 20 0:00	Ge 28:19	Disc 1, Track 31 2:49	53:33
3	Ge 28:20	Disc 1, Track 31 2:49	Ge 40:11	Disc 1, Track 43 1:16	50:56
4	Ge 40:12	Disc 1, Track 43 1:16	Ge 50:26	Disc 1, Track 53 3:50 (end)	49:08
5	Ex 1:1	Disc 1, Track 54 0:00	Ex 15:18	Disc 1, Track 69 3:11	61:27
6	Ex 15:19	Disc 1, Track 69 3:11	Ex 28:43	Disc 1, Track 82 5:55 (end)	53:52
7	Ex 29:1	Disc 1, Track 83 0:00	Ex 40:38	Disc 1, Track 94 3:58 (end)	53:10
8	Le 1:1	Disc 1, Track 95 0:00	Le 14:32	Disc 1, Track 109 4:54	61:45
9	Le 14:33	Disc 1, Track 109 4:54	Le 26:26	Disc 1, Track 121 3:40	57:51
10	Le 26:27	Disc 1, Track 121 3:40	Nu 8:14	Disc 1, Track 131 1:39	52:59
11	Nu 8:15	Disc 1, Track 131 1:39	Nu 21:7	Disc 1, Track 144 1:06	54:39
12	Nu 21:8	Disc 1, Track 144 1:06	Nu 32:19	Disc 1, Track 155 2:33	49:57
13	Nu 32:20	Disc 1, Track 155 2:33	Dt 7:26	Disc 1, Track 167 4:50(end)	59:32
14	Dt 8:1	Disc 1, Track 168 0:00	Dt 23:11	Disc 1, Track 183 1:30	62:38
15	Dt 23:12	Disc 1, Track 183 1:30	Dt 34:12	Disc 1, Track 194 1:54 (end)	61:28
16	Jos 1:1	Disc 2, Track 1 0:00	Jos 14:15	Disc 2, Track 15 2:32 (end)	56:09
17	Jos 15:1	Disc 2, Track 16 0:00	Jdg 3:27	Disc 2, Track 29 3:38	56:26
18	Jdg 3:28	Disc 2, Track 29 3:38	Jdg 15:12	Disc 2, Track 41 1:52	51:10
19	Jdg 15:13	Disc 2, Track 41 1:52	1Sa 2:29	Disc 2, Track 55 4:36	51:49
20	1Sa 2:30	Disc 2, Track 55 4:36	1Sa 15:35	Disc 2, Track 68 5:14 (end)	51:17
21	1Sa 16:1	Disc 2, Track 69 0:00	1Sa 28:19	Disc 2, Track 81 2:53	53:42
22	1Sa 28:20	Disc 2, Track 81 2:53	2Sa 12:10	Disc 2, Track 97 1:43	52:26
23	2Sa 12:11	Disc 2, Track 97 1:43	2Sa 22:18	Disc 2, Track 107 1:58	53:17
24	2Sa 22:19	Disc 2, Track 107 1:58	1Ki 7:37	Disc 2, Track 117 5:08	52:04
25	1Ki 7:38	Disc 2, Track 117 5:08	1Ki 16:20	Disc 2, Track 126 3:07	51:50
26	1Ki 16:21	Disc 2, Track 126 3:07	2Ki 4:37	Disc 2, Track 137 5:05	53:18
27	2Ki 4:38	Disc 2, Track 137 5:05	2Ki 15:26	Disc 2, Track 148 4:11	53:49
28	2Ki 15:27	Disc 2, Track 148 4:11	2Ki 25:30	Disc 2, Track 158 4:50 (end)	51:29
29	1Ch 1:1	Disc 2, Track 159 0:00	1Ch 9:44	Disc 2, Track 168 6:05 (end)	52:06
30	1Ch 10:1	Disc 2, Track 169 0:00	1Ch 23:32	Disc 2, Track 182 4:28 (end)	52:21
31	1Ch 24:1	Disc 2, Track 183 0:00	2Ch 7:10	Disc 2, Track 196 1:47	52:40
32	2Ch 7:11	Disc 2, Track 196 1:47	2Ch 23:15	Disc 2, Track 212 2:54	53:32

Day	Start Verse	Start	End Verse	End	Run Time
33	2Ch 23:16	Disc 2, Track 212 2:54	2Ch 35:15	Disc 2, Track 224 2:49	54:27
34	2Ch 35:16	Disc 2, Track 224 2:49	Ez 10:44	Disc 3, Track 11 6:18 (end)	48:34
35	Ne 1:1	Disc 3, Track 12 0:00	Ne 13:14	Disc 3, Track 25 2:27	60:04
36	Ne 13:15	Disc 3, Track 25 2:27	Job 7:21	Disc 3, Track 44 2:24 (end)	52:32
37	Job 8:1	Disc 3, Track 45 0:00	Job 24:25	Disc 3, Track 61 3:01 (end)	41:49
38	Job 25:1	Disc 3, Track 62 0:00	Job 41:34	Disc 3, Track 78 2:57 (end)	42:55
39	Job 42:1	Disc 3, Track 79 0:00	Ps 24:10	Disc 3, Track 104 1:08 (end)	39:37
40	Ps 25:1	Disc 3, Track 105 0:00	Ps 45:14	Disc 3, Track 125 2:07	41:20
41	Ps 45:15	Disc 3, Track 125 2:07	Ps 69:21	Disc 3, Track 149 2:36	42:11
42	Ps 69:22	Disc 3, Track 149 2:36	Ps 89:13	Disc 3, Track 169 1:35	45:20
43	Ps 89:14	Disc 3, Track 169 1:35	Ps 108:13	Disc 3, Track 188 1:18 (end)	43:31
44	Ps 109:1	Disc 3, Track 189 0:00	Ps 134:3	Disc 3, Track 214 0:18 (end)	41:00
45	Ps 135:1	Disc 3, Track 215 0:00	Pr 6:35	Disc 3, Track 237 3:17 (end)	41:00
46	Pr 7:1	Disc 3, Track 238 0:00	Pr 20:21	Disc 3, Track 251 2:07	39:00
47	Pr 20:22	Disc 3, Track 251 2:07	Ecc 2:26	Disc 3, Track 265 3:50 (end)	42:11
48	Ecc 3:1	Disc 3, Track 266 0:00	SoS 8:14	Disc 3, Track 284 2:01 (end)	41:07
49	Isa 1:1	Disc 3, Track 285 0:00	Isa 13:22	Disc 3, Track 299 3:10 (end)	43:59
50	Isa 14:1	Disc 3, Track 300 0:00	Isa 28:29	Disc 3, Track 314 5:16 (end)	44:40
51	Isa 29:1	Disc 3, Track 315 0:00	Isa 41:18	Disc 3, Track 327 3:06	45:33
52	Isa 41:19	Disc 3, Track 327 3:06	Isa 52:12	Disc 3, Track 338 2:17	45:33
53	Isa 52:13	Disc 3, Track 338 2:17	Isa 66:18	Disc 3, Track 352 3:55	44:07
54	Isa 66:19	Disc 3, Track 352 3:55	Jer 10:13	Disc 4, Track 11 1:55	46:56
55	Jer 10:14	Disc 4, Track 11 1:55	Jer 23:8	Disc 4, Track 24 1:30	45:51
56	Jer 23:9	Disc 4, Track 24 1:30	Jer 33:22	Disc 4, Track 34 3:42	49:48
57	Jer 33:23	Disc 4, Track 34 3:42	Jer 47:7	Disc 4, Track 48 1:08 (end)	46:32
58	Jer 48:1	Disc 4, Track 49 0:00	La 1:22	Disc 4, Track 55 4:59 (end)	40:50
59	La 2:1	Disc 4, Track 56 0:00	Eze 12:20	Disc 4, Track 72 3:23	61:52
60	Eze 12:21	Disc 4, Track 72 3:23	Eze 23:39	Disc 4, Track 83 6:19	60:28
61	Eze 23:40	Disc 4, Track 83 6:19	Eze 35:15	Disc 4, Track 95 2:41 (end)	56:38
62	Eze 36:1	Disc 4, Track 96 0:00	Eze 47:12	Disc 4, Track 107 2:01	59:17
63	Eze 47:13	Disc 4, Track 107 2:01	Da 8:27	Disc 4, Track 117 4:19 (end)	48:57
64	Da 9:1	Disc 4, Track 118 0:00	Hos 13:6	Disc 4, Track 135 0:55	45:21
65	Hos 13:7	Disc 4, Track 135 0:55	Am 9:10	Disc 4, Track 150 2:11	40:20
66	Am 9:11	Disc 4, Track 150 2:11	Nah 3:19	Disc 4, Track 169 3:10 (end)	44:32
67	Hab 1:1	Disc 4, Track 171 0:00	Zec 10:12	Disc 4, Track 191 2:08 (end)	51:25
68	Zec 11:1	Disc 4, Track 192 0:00	Mt 4:25	Disc 5, Track 6 3:33 (end)	38:12

Day	Start Verse	Start	End Verse	End	Run Time
69	Mt 5:1	Disc 5, Track 7 0:00	Mt 15:39	Disc 5, Track 17 2:26 (end)	59:28
70	Mt 16:1	Disc 5, Track 18 0:00	Mt 26:56	Disc 5, Track 28 7:42	59:07
71	Mt 26:57	Disc 5, Track 28 7:42	Mk 9:13	Disc 5, Track 40 1:42	57:19
72	Mk 9:14	Disc 5, Track 40 1:42	Lk 1:80	Disc 5, Track 49 9:31 (end)	57:10
73	Lk 2:1	Disc 5, Track 50 0:00	Lk 9:62	Disc 5, Track 57 8:50 (end)	57:12
74	Lk 10:1	Disc 5, Track 58 0:00	Lk 20:19	Disc 5, Track 68 2:33	59:43
75	Lk 20:20	Disc 5, Track 68 2:33	Jn 5:47	Disc 5, Track 78 5:49 (end)	57:40
76	Jn 6:1	Disc 5, Track 79 0:00	Jn 15:17	Disc 5, Track 88 2:27	56:46
77	Jn 15:18	Disc 5, Track 88 2:27	Ac 6:7	Disc 6, Track 7 1:02	50:54
78	Ac 6:8	Disc 6, Track 7 1:02	Ac 16:37	Disc 6, Track 17 5:01	50:42
79	Ac 16:38	Disc 6, Track 17 5:01	Ac 28:16	Disc 6, Track 29 2:07	55:07
80	Ac 28:17	Disc 6, Track 29 2:07	Ro 14:23	Disc 6, Track 44 3:27 (end)	59:54
81	Ro 15:1	Disc 6, Track 45 0:00	1Co 14:40	Disc 6, Track 61 5:19 (end)	59:01
82	1Co 15:1	Disc 6, Track 62 0:00	Gal 3:25	Disc 6, Track 81 3:49	61:13
83	Gal 3:26	Disc 6, Track 81 3:49	Col 4:18	Disc 6, Track 101 2:25 (end)	61:31
84	1Th 1:1	Disc 6, Track 102 0:00	Phm 25	Disc 6, Track 129 3:01 (end)	61:57
85	Heb 1:1	Disc 6, Track 130 0:00	Jas 3:12	Disc 6, Track 147 1:46	56:36
86	Jas 3:13	Disc 6, Track 147 1:46	3Jn 14	Disc 6, Track 169 2:06 (end)	59:25
87	Jude 1	Disc 6, Track 170 0:00	Rev 17:18	Disc 6, Track 189 3:35 (end)	62:03
88	Rev 18:1	Disc 6, Track 190 0:00	Rev 22:21	Disc 6, Track 194 4:02 (end)	20:13
89					
90					